USING

COMMON WORSHIP:

Daily Prayer

USING
COMMON WORSHIP:
Daily Prayer

A Practical Guide to the New Services

Jeremy Fletcher and Gilly Myers

Introduction by Andrew Burnham

Church House Publishing
Church House,
Great Smith Street,
London SW1P 3NZ

ISBN   0 7151 2065 4

Published 2002 by Church House Publishing and *Praxis*

All quoted material in boxes is from
Common Worship: Daily Prayer (Preliminary Edition),
Church House Publishing, 2002
Copyright © The Archbishops' Council 2002

Telephone   020 7898 1557
Fax   020 7898 1449
Email   *copyright@c-of-e.org.uk*

Cover design
by   Church House Publishing

Printed by   The Cromwell Press Ltd, Trowbridge, Wiltshire

Typeset in   11pt Sabon and 11.5pt Gill Sans
                by Pioneer Associates (Graphic) Ltd, Perthshire

Contents

What is *Praxis*?

Praxis was formed in 1990, sponsored by the Liturgical Commission of the Church of England, the Alcuin Club, and the Group for the Renewal of Worship (GROW). It exists to provide and support liturgical education in the Church of England.

Its aims are:

- to enrich the practice and understanding of worship in the Church of England;
- to serve congregations and clergy in their exploration of the call to worship;
- to provide a forum in which different worshipping traditions can meet and interact.

The name *Praxis* comes from the Greek word for action. It emphasizes our practical concerns and conveys our conviction that worship is a primary expression of the Christian faith.

Praxis runs an annual programme of day conferences and residential workshops around the country, organized either centrally or by *Praxis* regions (informal networks of diocesan liturgical committees).

You can find out more about *Praxis* from our web site:
www.sarum.ac.uk/praxis/

For a copy of the *Praxis* programme and details of how to affiliate, contact the *Praxis* office:

Praxis
St Matthew's House
20 Great Peter Street
LONDON
SW1P 2BU
Tel: 020 7222 3704
Fax: 020 7233 0255
Email: praxis@London.com

Foreword to the series

Those who produced the *Common Worship* services wanted to provide liturgical resources that encourage worshipping communities to take account of the pastoral needs of the congregation and the mission imperative of worship that engages with the surrounding culture.

The synodical process has, rightly, focused on the texts, the structures and the rubrics. But the services will only come to life and reach their potential as living encounters with God in the nitty-gritty of worship in parish churches, hospital and prison chapels, school halls and other centres of worship. *Praxis* was set up by the Liturgical Commission in partnership with The Group for the Renewal of Worship (GROW) and the Alcuin Club to foster just such a practical approach to liturgy – working at grass roots level to support real churches who are seeking to make their regular worship better. *Praxis* has been running training events and courses to this end for ten years and it is a great step forward to see the combination of deeper understanding and better practice coming together in print.

The *Using Common Worship* series is a creative partnership between *Praxis* and Church House Publishing which will help all of us to make the most of *Common Worship*. Each volume bridges the gap between the bare texts and the experience of using those texts in worship. Full of practical advice, backed up with the underlying thinking from members of the Liturgical Commission, these books will be a valuable tool to put alongside the *Common Worship* volumes on the shelves of every worship leader in the Church of England.

✠ *David Sarum*
Chairman of the Liturgical Commission

Introduction
Andrew Burnham

An overview

Everyone who reads this book will know of the existence of
Morning and Evening Prayer. Some of us will also be familiar
with the daily prayer of religious communities, which follows a
similar pattern. But where does it come from, this daily prayer of
the Church, the 'Office' (see Appendix 1, p. 116), and how has it
developed? The purpose of this Introduction is to provide some
historical and liturgical background to the most recent revision of
the Church of England's Office, to be found in *Common
Worship: Daily Prayer*. The chapters that follow will focus on
how to make the best use of these opportunities for prayer.

It is tempting for the historian to trace the Church's daily prayer
('the Office') back through *The Book of Common Prayer* and
back through the monastic offices of the medieval Church to
some simpler forms which, themselves, derived from the worship
of the synagogue. What else would the Lord have encountered at
the synagogue at Capernaum (Mark 1.21) or Nazareth (Luke
4.16) other than the Church's Office at its simplest? Psalms and
canticles and scripture readings and prayers: the simpler the
Office, it follows, the closer it must be to the services described in
the gospels and, indeed, the Acts of the Apostles (e.g. Acts 1.14,
2.42, 4.24, 12.5,12).

There must be something in this. Things do become gradually
more complicated as time goes on. The services of the synagogue
and the home in the first century AD presumably included psalms
and canticles and prayers as well as the Scripture reading we
know about from Luke 4. We do hear of Jesus and his disciples
singing psalms (Matthew 26.30 and parallels). We know that
Jesus retired to the desert or hills to pray (Mark 1.36). Yet we

must not presume that, because synagogue worship is older than church worship, the Church derives its material from the Synagogue. The visitor to a modern synagogue will note many similarities between Jewish and Christian worship – furniture and fittings, ceremonial and symbol, texts and translations – but it would be wrong to assume that in every instance the Church was copying the Synagogue. In fact, the Church was as surely an influence on the Synagogue as the Synagogue on the Church: the increasing Jewish use of candles in place of oil lamps is one example of this.

Another problem with tracing things back to the first-century synagogue is that we know very little about the worship of the Church in the period before AD 313. That was the year in which the Emperor Constantine's Edict of Milan started the process of state approval for Christianity in the Roman Empire. Prior to that, in many places and under several emperors, Christianity was very much an underground movement. Once Christianity became publicly permitted and, gradually, the established religion of the Roman Empire, we know much more about everything, including the celebration of daily prayer.

A particular hazard for Westerners in tracing back traditions of daily prayer is that much of the flowering of the Office was in the East. Some of our perceptions – that the Office is mainly cerebral or clerical, or that we always use the Benedictus in the morning and the Magnificat in the evening – collapse when we see what goes on in the various examples of the Eastern Office. As we shall discover, there were town and country traditions, the one more popular, the other more monastic. We shall see too that the Office in the West has been so monastic in character that it has been hard for people to join in with it, at any rate on a casual basis. This is true not only of the Roman Office, with its labyrinthine books, but also of *The Book of Common Prayer* and its lengthy lectionaries.

Various dilemmas face those with the task of constructing or revising the Office. One dilemma is that a very simple and accessible Office, in which a newcomer can easily share, is likely to become too banal for those who use it for years on end. *The Book of Common Prayer* dealt with this by setting the variables of an annual cycle of Scripture (four chapters a day), a monthly cycle of psalmody (an average of five psalms a day) and a weekly collect within the otherwise unchanging framework of Morning and Evening Prayer.

Another dilemma is posed by Bible reading: do we keep to 'purple passages', ideal for the new Christian and casual visitor, or do we risk plunging people unprepared into the genealogies of the first few chapters of 1 Chronicles or the apocalyptic battles of The Revelation to John? None of the main lectionary schemes to date – *The Book of Common Prayer* lectionaries, *The Alternative Service Book 1980* lectionary, the *Celebrating Common Prayer* lectionary – has been suitable for the casual visitor or occasional user.

A third dilemma concerns the presence or absence of a congregation. One of the conventions of the Office is its corporate expression. Even for individual recitation the device of Versicles and Responses, for example, is maintained: 'O Lord open thou *our* lips: and *our* mouth shall shew forth thy praise.' When there is a congregation present, new criteria jostle for attention: the lighting of candles and the singing of canticles, which direction people face and whether they sit, stand or kneel, for instance. It then becomes sensible to move from the monastic towards the popular, with something more like the old Byzantine 'People's Office' (see below, page 10) than the classic Roman Office (see below, page 12).

What seems to be common to the praying of the Office is that, whatever the circumstances, individuals take their places in the never-ceasing cycle of prayer (1 Thessalonians 5.17, see also Luke 18.1, 21.36, Ephesians 6.18), the Church's offering of praise. It is corporate prayer and not private praying and, as the well-known evening hymn, 'The Day Thou Gavest' by J. Ellerton, so memorably puts it, it is an activity that goes on simultaneously all over the world:

> As o'er each continent and island
> The dawn leads on another day,
> The voice of prayer is never silent,
> Nor dies the strain of praise away.
>
> The sun that bids us rest is waking
> Our brethren 'neath the western sky,
> And hour by hour fresh lips are making
> Thy wondrous doings heard on high.

We are not only linked geographically, we are also linked with a long tradition: the cycle of praise is centuries old. We are not engaged in anything new; we are taking our place within the history and tradition of a pilgrim people, part of whose reason for existence is to share in that living sacrifice of spiritual worship in which we are transformed by the renewing of our minds (Romans 12.1-2).

Experiments with the Office in the 1960s and 1970s

There have been many attempts in recent times to make the Office serve its true purpose more effectively. Among these have been the authorized services of the Church of England. There were a couple of tidying-up operations on the Prayer Book Office in the 1960s. Under the Prayer Book (Alternative and Other Services) Measure 1965, the Liturgical Commission produced the Alternative Services Series 1 (1965) and Series 2 (completed 1962, authorized 1968). These were, essentially, conservative revisions of *The Book of Common Prayer*. It became possible, for instance, to begin the Office with 'O Lord open thou our lips', instead of 'When the wicked man . . .'!

In Series 2 Morning Prayer – which was still in traditional language – the Te Deum and the Benedictus were swapped round. Cranmer, the compiler of the First and Second Prayer Books of King Edward VI, had conflated medieval Matins (with its Te Deum) and Lauds (with its Benedictus), leaving the canticles in that order. Series 2 took the view that the sequence of the canticles in the Christian story was more important than their sequence in the medieval Office and so the Benedictus, a hymn of praise about the Incarnation, came after the psalms and Old Testament reading, and the Te Deum, a hymn of praise about the glory of God and the exalted Christ, came after the New Testament reading.

The Church Assembly also discussed the (ecumenical) Joint Liturgical Group's work: *The Daily Office*, 1968 (published as *The Daily Office Revised* by SPCK in 1978).

In the light of these experiments a new Office emerged from the Church of England. Published first as *Common Prayer 1970* and then, more fully, as *Alternative Services Second Series (Revised)*

Morning and Evening Prayer, also in 1970, the new proposals took final shape as *Morning and Evening Prayer Series 3* in 1975 and were published thereafter in *The Alternative Service Book 1980* (ASB).

ASB Morning and Evening Prayer – available in longer and shorter forms – were scarcely revolutionary, except in their use of modern language. The main innovation was that a variety of canticles could be used. The Lucan Canticles – the Benedictus, Magnificat and Nunc dimittis – took their place within a longer list. Cranmer's achievement had been ever-changing Scripture lessons, embedded like glittering jewels in the unchanging settings of Morning and Evening Prayer. In the new office there was a greater variety of jewels and less setting. If ASB Morning and Evening Prayer caught on less well than the Liturgical Commission had hoped, it was, perhaps, because they were too 'public' in feel for private use and too inflexible for those who wanted to use them publicly. The work on the Office felt like a job half done, certainly as compared with the work on the ASB Rite A Order for Holy Communion.

Meanwhile the Roman *Liturgy of the Hours* (*Liturgia Hororum*) (1971)[1] emerged. Its expressed hope (General Instruction on the Liturgy of the Hours, n. 27) was that

> wherever groups of the laity are gathered and whatever the purpose which has brought them together, such as prayer or the apostolate, they are encouraged to recite the Church's Office by celebrating part of the Liturgy of the Hours.

The Roman Office is intended for use wherever the Roman Rite prevails. Anglicans, however, produce their liturgies on a provincial basis and so each of the Anglican service books – in Australia, New Zealand, South Africa and so on – has its own form of the Office. There are family resemblances, of course, but whereas Roman Catholics are united in their prayers (with, however, a diversity of language), Anglicans are united in their praying (with a diversity of forms and languages).

Experiments with the Office in the 1990s

Apart from the authorized services, informal versions have abounded. Some of these sprang from a fascination with Taizé, others from a fascination with the new Roman vernacular Office. *Celebrating Common Prayer* is, perhaps, the best-known of the latter (published as *Celebrating Common Prayer* and in a Franciscan version as *The Daily Office SSF*, both Mowbray, 1992). The genius of CCP, as it is usually known, is that its Morning and Evening Prayer can follow the Cranmerian (and ASB-type) shape:

Opening praise

Psalms

Old Testament reading

Canticle

New Testament reading

Canticle

Prayers

Equally, however, Morning and Evening Prayer can follow the Roman shape:

Opening praise

Psalms and Canticle

Reading

Gospel Canticle

Prayers

Those who use CCP – or its Franciscan version – are rewarded with the opportunity to use a proper Office Book, markers and all! The spirituality of the breviary, the portable office book, invented by the Franciscans in the middle of the thirteenth century, is now easily available to reformed Christians. Like the Roman *Liturgy of the Hours*, there is provision for prayer at midday and for Compline. Unlike the Roman *Liturgy of the Hours*, CCP is only one volume.

As regards format and development, CCP stands in the same relationship to *Common Worship: Daily Prayer* as that of *Morning and Evening Prayer Series 3* to *The Alternative Service Book 1980*. The difference is that CCP, despite its popularity, remains an unofficial collection. Warmly commended by the Archbishop of Canterbury, it is, nevertheless, outside the provision of the Prayer Book (Alternative and Other Services) Measures. It contains neither 'alternative services' nor material 'commended by the House of Bishops'.

In 1994 the Church of England authorized an ingenious new outline service – A Service of the Word (*A Service of the Word and Affirmations of Faith*, CHP, 1994). As a result, any service which conforms to the requirements of that outline can be considered authorized. More than that, A Service of the Word can be used canonically as a 'statutory service'. The happy result was that from 1994, material from *Celebrating Common Prayer* could be used legally for Morning and Evening Prayer and for the first part of the Holy Communion in parish churches.

A Service of the Word was originally seen as an outline for non-eucharistic services on a Sunday. It soon became clear, however, that it would also make a good framework for the Daily Office on weekdays. To facilitate this, when it was re-authorized in 1999 for use in *Common Worship*, the Notes were amended so that the use of Prayers of Penitence and a Creed or authorized Affirmation of Faith were only required 'at the principal service on Sundays and Principal Holy Days'. This brought daily prayer based on, for instance, *Celebrating Common Prayer* under the umbrella of authorized services.

In the late 1990s the Liturgical Commission of the Church of England took a close interest in *The Durham Office*, an experiment within the diocese of Durham. A number of seasonal booklets were accumulated and stored, at the experimental stage, in a shoe-box; these later formed the basis of a published collection of booklets with their own storage box. The booklets were simple to use and solved the problems of accessibility versus richness, the needs of the newcomer and those of the experienced user. Meanwhile there has been much public interest in so-called 'Celtic' offices. Again these have a simplicity and directness and an emphasis on creation, the elements and the wonders of nature (although the incomparable riches of the psalms need no augmenting in any of these respects). Almost every book of prayers, of which there have been many in the last decade, has included its own Office and there have been several popular office books such as the American Benedictine *Work of God* (The Liturgical Press, Collegeville, 1997) and *A Week of Simple Offices: CR* (Community of the Resurrection, Mirfield).

Common Worship: Daily Prayer

Any fresh endeavour in constructing the Office needs to produce a service that is

- simple to use (though complex enough to bear endless repetition)

- corporate in feel (though not exclusively monastic)

- convincing as a part of the universal offering of praise.

For some, this last requirement has led them to use only such forms as command widespread allegiance – for instance, the Roman *Liturgy of the Hours* (*Liturgia Hororum*). For others, the Office needs to be complex but, as in the East, taking part consists not in attempting 'to do it all' but in treating the Daily Office as a treasure-house. There is this jewel, and that one, to look at and use as a start to contemplation. A psalm, a seasonal responsory, a verse or two of Scripture: this is all you need and for this the Office books are an anthology of devotion rather than a programme of prayers to be got through. Indeed, for some the whole idea of 'the Office' has been unhelpful. 'Daily prayer' has meant Christians throughout the ages and throughout the world reading the Scriptures and saying their prayers. Lectionaries and schemes of intercession are aids to Bible reading and prayer but they can easily become – as so often they have done in the history of the Office – a legalistic straitjacket.

Those for whom the Office is essentially a form of prayer used throughout the world will not immediately be satisfied by *Common Worship: Daily Prayer*. If, however, it catches the imagination like *Celebrating Common Prayer*, it will be used by a wide and international group of English-speaking Christians and not just by English Anglicans. More than that, it specifically caters for those for whom the Office – and indeed the very notion of 'an office' – seems impossibly restrictive.

Common Worship: Daily Prayer begins not with Morning Prayer nor even with Evening Prayer. It begins with Prayer During the

Day. In other words it starts with the assumption that there is some praying to be done day by day and that this task will be approached in different ways and at different times of day. Christians throughout the ages and throughout the world are united in the priority they give to prayer and Bible reading but this will be expressed in different ways in different cultures. For some, Prayer During the Day will function effectively as a 'Day Office' to which Night Prayer (or Compline) is the natural complement. For others Prayer During the Day will function as an 'Office of Readings' – a 'Quiet Time' during which the main daily reading of Scripture takes place and serious space is created for meditation and prayer. For others Prayer During the Day will be a short 'Midday Office', a pause in the middle of the day that complements the main praying and reading which happens at Morning and Evening Prayer in the time-honoured Anglican way.

For some, provision of Morning and Evening Prayer is all that is needed. It is, after all, the pattern of Cranmer and *The Alternative Service Book 1980*. They may regard the addition of Prime and Compline to the Prayer Book in 1928 and the Midday Office and Compline in *Celebrating Common Prayer* as 'high church' and retrograde, moving from the brilliant synthesis of Cranmer's public services back towards the more monastic pattern that the archbishop had so imaginatively quarried. However, *Common Worship: Daily Prayer* works very successfully as a traditional two-office scheme and the psalms and readings of the new lectionaries can be used for this without adaptation.

A deeper perspective

The history of the Office is immensely complex and rich.[2] Half a dozen snapshots, each of which illustrates the continuing debate within the tradition, may provide a deeper perspective.

Town and country at the beginning of the fifth century

By the beginning of the fifth century two patterns of Office – city and desert, town and country – had emerged. The nun Egeria, travelling from France or Spain, gives us a full description of her visit to Jerusalem and the Office as she encounters it:

- It is a city event.

- It is led by ordained ministers and involving the whole congregation.

- There is praise and intercession.

- The psalms and canticles of praise are chosen for their appropriateness.

- The lamps are ceremonially lit at nightfall and incense is burnt.

Compare with that the description by John Cassian, a monk from Gaul who visited Egypt, of the Office he encounters:

- It is a desert event.

- It is celebrated by individuals without any distinction of ministry or ecclesiastical office.

- There is silent meditation.

- All 150 psalms are used and the whole Bible read as 'food for thought'.

- The community adopts similar postures but there are no ceremonies.

There had been a call in third-century Alexandria for 'perfect Christians' to move beyond set times to continuous prayer. The emergence of the Egyptian Desert Fathers, hermits living close enough to each other to form what were effectively communities of individuals, is the supreme example of the result of this call to move from town to country ways of prayer.

The Eastern Office

The remoteness of Eastern Christianity, from the vantage point of the West, has meant that the strength of the 'town' Office has sometimes been underestimated. The old Byzantine Office, as it developed in the fifth and sixth centuries, lasted in some regions for the best part of a thousand years. It was a 'People's Office' and it survived in Constantinople until the city was attacked by

Latin crusaders in 1204. It lasted considerably longer in Thessalonica, until the Turkish invasion in the fifteenth century. In this 'chanted Office', as one contemporary bishop called it, there were processions from the narthex (the vestibule) to the ambo (a raised platform) then on to the sanctuary. There was the throwing open of doors and, on certain evenings, the ceremonial lighting of lamps. Incense was in great supply and there was much singing of psalms. The robed participants provided for themselves and others a spectacle of beauty and the Christian pilgrimage from darkness to light, from death to life, was imaginatively enacted.

After the attack on Constantinople, the 'People's Office' gave way to a more complex Office which had originated in Palestine and had been developing in monasteries over hundreds of years. The resulting 'Byzantine Office', which is still in use, has up to fourteen offices a day, with 'inter-hours' interspersed amongst the 'hours'. In it, a fully developed 'monastic' Office encases, as it were, a 'cathedral' Office, with vestments, ceremonial and music all playing a part, not least for the *lucernarium*, the high point of Vespers, when the lamps are lit and incense burned.

There is a similar drama of Sundays and feasts, when the Gospels are enthroned and venerated in the centre of the church and bread is distributed. There are points in the Office where the *felonion* (the chasuble) is put on and there are points where it is taken off – a moving in and out of 'cathedral' mode, all within a monastic context.

The massive treasury of canons and odes – the hymnody of the Orthodox Church – is an adornment of the truths of Scripture but, surprisingly, the reading of Scripture plays a very small part indeed. There are Scripture readings on principal feasts and during Lent but not otherwise.

The whole Office amounts to an intricate patchwork which parishes have to adapt to their needs. Parish churches lack the resources to celebrate the Office in full, so they do what they can; and in the same way individuals participate by dropping in and out. Through the intricacy of hymns and psalms and litanies and prayers, the impression created is of never-ceasing prayer and the life of eternity.

The Western Office

The Western Office emerges in the sixth century along with two monastic rules: the Rule of the Master and, twenty years later, the Rule of St Benedict (*c.* 540). St Benedict himself describes the spirituality of his Office:

> 'Seven times a day have I praised thee,' said the prophet [Psalm 119.164]. We shall perform this consecrated number of seven if we offer prayer (the duty of our profession) at the hours of Lauds, Prime, Terce, Sext, None, Vespers, and Compline. It was of these day hours that he said: 'Seven times a day have I praised thee.' Elsewhere the same prophet makes mention of the night office, 'at midnight I rose to confess thee.' At these times, therefore, let us render praise to our creator 'for the judgments of his justice' – that is, Lauds, Prime, Terce, Sext, None, Vespers, Compline: and let us rise at night to confess to him.[3]

There is austerity but realism:

> It is a mean devotion if monks should in a week sing less than the whole Psalter with the usual canticles. We read that our holy fathers bravely recited the Psalter in a single day; God grant that we, their degenerate sons, may do the like in seven.[4]

From Benedict comes not only the whole Western monastic office tradition but the Roman Office, as used by secular clergy and in parishes, and in due course the reformed offices of *The Book of Common Prayer*. There is much more reading of Scripture in the Western Office than in the Eastern Office – particularly during the night, at 'nocturns' – but far fewer hymns. Whereas the Byzantine Office continues to have its 'cathedral' features, set amidst its monastic structure, the Roman Office (whether Benedictine or not) makes little use of hierarchy, ceremonial and movement. People sit in rows and remain in rows. Solemn celebrations of Vespers and sometimes Lauds make some use of 'cathedral' features – the celebrants wear coloured copes and the altar is censed at the singing of the Gospel Canticle – but such celebrations are uncommon. More commonly the monks – and sometimes the congregation as well – are in choir stalls. Half face north and half face south. To the east is the altar and to the west is often the lectern. It is as if the People's Office of Constantinople were to be celebrated solely on the ambo, and meditation and antiphonal recitation have replaced pilgrimage and ceremonial. In abbeys and medieval cathedrals, indeed, the Office takes place in the distance – beyond the screen, 'in choir'. The Office is something that the clergy and religious do: it is their prayer, of course, but it is more than that; it is their formation and their education. This was no more so than when the scarcity of liturgical books made it inevitable that the Office should be sung largely by heart.

Quinones and Cranmer

When the Council of Trent in 1568 abolished all forms of Office less than 200 years old, it was not only centralizing the Roman Rite but also setting about its work of liturgical reform. Of greatest interest to us is not that reform but one of the experiments that pre-dated it by thirty odd years. The breviary of the Spanish Franciscan, Cardinal Quinones, was produced by order of the Pope. The reforms of this 'Breviary of the Holy Cross' (1535) were too far-reaching for the Council of Trent. Their time would come 400 years later but meanwhile they greatly influenced the English Reformer, Thomas Cranmer. Ironically, Quinones had taken an active interest in the question of Henry VIII's divorce and had defended the interests of Catherine of Aragon.

Quinones' reforms included the abolishing of antiphons and responsories, psalmody arranged to be read in course once a week, the reduction of saints' days and the reading of nearly all the Bible in course each year. The office hymn was brought forward to the beginning of each 'hour'. Cranmer went further:

- The monastic offices – seven for the day and one for the night – were reduced to two, Morning Prayer and Evening Prayer.

- The psalms were to be read in course once a month.

- The Old Testament was to be read in course once a year.

- The New Testament was to be read in course twice a year.

- The services were to be in English.

If, in the Western Office, the 'cathedral' aspect of daily prayer had largely disappeared in favour of the 'monastic', Quinones and Cranmer did little to revive it. The problem of lay participation – as we would call it – had been tackled in the late Middle Ages. Books of Hours had appeared for lay people to use, with the penitential psalms, votive offices of the Blessed Virgin, the Litany of the Saints and other such devotions. The ringing of the Angelus bell and the saying of the Rosary had become increasingly popular and, alongside the *Lectio Divina* of the clergy – reading and learning by heart Scripture and the writings of the Fathers – the movement of mystical piety known as the '*Devotio moderna*' had spread like wildfire among clergy and laity. *Devotio moderna* was intensely human and real and inspired both *The Imitation of Christ* by Thomas à Kempis and Ignatius of Loyola's *Spiritual Exercises*. Another fruit of the *Devotio moderna*, *A Manual of Prayers*, ran to a hundred editions between 1583 and the middle of the nineteenth century. All of this flourished alongside what remained, even with Quinones' and Cranmer's reforms, an essentially 'monastic' office. Indeed, it could be said that popular devotion developed its own momentum because the Church's Office was so clerical.

Cranmer's Prayer Book – or rather its revision in 1662 – held sway throughout the following centuries. The 1928 Prayer Book, defeated by parliament, suggested very few reforms to the Office and it is surprising how popular the Tudor reform remains. Choral Matins may have almost disappeared but Choral Evensong is alive and well in 'quires and places where they sing'. Many parish churches which have used the most modern available Order for Holy Communion these last forty years still persevere with Prayer Book Evensong. There are churches which offer 'Solemn Evensong and Benediction', a 'cathedral' version of the Office, with lights and incense and eucharistic devotions, and there are still more which use just one psalm, chosen for its suitability to the time or season – another 'cathedral' feature. For the most part, however, Cranmer's Office, as it has been celebrated this last 450 years, remains 'monastic'. Its priorities may be innately clerical – four long readings a day, the psalter once a month – but it has been remarkably successful. Samuel Pepys took part in 6 a.m. Matins, which was a daily service, and George Herbert, according to his biographer Izaak Walton, recruited most of his parishioners to take part in daily Morning and Evening Prayer.[5]

Although there was considerable decline in weekday celebration of the Office in England towards the end of the eighteenth century, the Tractarians enthusiastically revived – and supplemented – the Office of *The Book of Common Prayer*. An instance of such supplements was the material produced at Cuddesdon College. Generations of students owed much of their spirituality to *Prayers in use at Cuddesdon College*, last reprinted in 1929, or to its successor, *The Cuddesdon Office Book*, published privately in 1940 and eventually published by the Oxford University Press in 1962. The offices of Prime, Terce, Sext, None and Compline, with propers and litanies, helped ordinands from this college, at any rate, to enjoy the full diet of a monastic office and an enriched 'kalendar with college memorials'.

Liturgy of the Hours (1971)

The reform of the Roman liturgy, initiated by the Second Vatican Council and completed, for the most part, by the early 1970s, was the most radical reform since the 1570s. It says something about the development of Western culture that Roman Catholics and Anglicans alike were able to maintain liturgical stability for 400 years until the 1960s, when a period of intense change completely altered the liturgical landscape of both churches. Other churches – except the Orthodox, where all is said to be unchanging – will have similar stories, but there are striking similarities between the collapse of Roman uniformity – at least linguistically – and the dismantling of the liturgical consensus of the Anglican Communion.

The new Roman Office, in a vernacular language, was, in other respects, not strikingly different from what went before. Three significant changes are readily identifiable, however. Firstly, the office of the night – often celebrated literally during the night in monasteries – became 'The Office of Readings', a study office of longer psalms and biblical and non-biblical readings. (The non-biblical readings are from the Fathers and from writings by, and about, the saints). This 'Office of Readings' may be celebrated at any time of day, to suit the user or community.

Secondly, the five minor offices of Prime, Terce, Sext, None and Compline are much reduced. Prime, which had often jostled with Lauds in its timing anyway, was suppressed. Compline was kept for use at the end of the day. The three remaining offices were contracted into 'Prayer During the Day', which can be adapted, according to preference, for use as a mid-morning office, a midday office or a mid-afternoon office, or expanded, by way of supplementary psalmody, into a full monastic diet. The obligation to say Prayer During the Day is thus mitigated by flexibility as to when it is used.

Thirdly – and perhaps most significantly – the two offices of Lauds ('Morning Prayer') and Vespers ('Evening Prayer') – were refashioned as offices in which it was hoped the laity would take a full part. Just as Cranmer had worked hard for full-scale popular participation, so now the Second Vatican Council had the same ambition. Critics might argue that participation remains elusive and difficult to achieve, but there have undoubtedly been considerable successes in achieving what Anglicans would call 'Common Prayer' or, indeed, 'Common Worship'.

Celebrating daily prayer

The last of the snapshots catches what has been perhaps the least obvious and yet the most unifying picture of all. Generations of reformed Christians, of a variety of denominations, have continued to do what ordinary lay people before the Reformation did. They have been faithful in their prayers and have sought to be united with the Church's offering of praise not so much by the material they used – an office, a lectionary, a prayer scheme – as by the fact that they were doing it. For many Christians – including, increasingly, Roman Catholics – the daily 'Quiet Time' has been a time of Bible study and prayer. Much of the historical perspective has been concerned with the saying and singing of the Office, but this has been no more than part of the story. In conclusion, then, *Common Worship: Daily Prayer* will succeed insofar as it unites faithful people – whether members of the Church of England or not – in the task of daily prayer. That task is meditating on words that are 'sweeter than honey' (Psalm 119.103) so that our lips pour forth God's praise (cf. Psalm 119.171a).

1 A living tradition of daily prayer

Jeremy Fletcher

There are probably as many ways of praying daily as there are people who pray. Catering for these many patterns was one of the challenges faced by the compilers and writers of *Common Worship: Daily Prayer*. For example, clergy of the Church of England find themselves required by the Canons of the Church of England to say Morning and Evening Prayer on a daily basis.[1] Many lay people also use Morning or Evening Prayer or both as the basis of their pattern of personal devotion. Others are looking for a more flexible pattern of daily prayer and have concentrated their devotions on a midday office, or night prayer. Still others have adapted Morning or Evening Prayer to become a single office. And many have an existing pattern of devotion centred around the study of the Bible combined with intercession: the classic 'Quiet Time' of the evangelical tradition.

A new form of daily prayer in the Church of England

Andrew Burnham's introduction has shown how the habit of daily prayer has been a feature of Christian devotion from earliest times, and how the Anglican pattern of corporate prayer focused on two points of the day became the norm. *The Alternative Service Book 1980* hardly changed this pattern, providing little variation and no alternatives for the seasons of the Church's year. This compared unfavourably with the seasonal variety of the Communion service in the same book, supplemented later by books such as *Lent, Holy Week, Easter* and *The Promise of His Glory*. It was soon evident that this was an opportunity lost, because over the last twenty years a renewed interest in spirituality has combined with diverse and more pressured lifestyles to produce a multiplicity of patterns of prayer. Many recent publications have supported this variety of practice and the pre-eminent position of morning and evening as times for prayer has come under challenge.

When the Liturgical Commission's Daily Office Group sat down to start work on *Common Worship: Daily Prayer* it faced a number of challenges.

- To provide orders for Morning and Evening Prayer which would meet the need for seasonal variety and richness of provision.

- To respond to the broadening of patterns of prayer which had seen a revival of 'Celtic' spirituality, the growth of the retreat movement and a renewed interest in the monastic spiritual tradition.

- To provide patterns of prayer which would nourish the sustained prayer of members of communities in monasteries, convents and religious houses.

- To acknowledge the patterns of personal devotion based around reading and study of the Bible – the Quiet Time – which exist outside the 'office' tradition.

- To provide resources for prayer that would acknowledge that changed lifestyles prohibit worshippers attending daily prayer at set times in church, whilst still allowing them to be part of a community of prayer.

Common Worship: Daily Prayer – an outline

The result of the Daily Office Group's work was four patterns of prayer, each capable of adaptation to suit local use, but with a broad overall pattern.

- *Prayer During the Day* is the most flexible order: it can be used as an outline for personal Bible reading, a midday office, a simple office, or the basis of a personal pattern of prayer.

- *Morning and Evening Prayer* are more traditional patterns of prayer, which can be simplified or made more elaborate according to local need. They relate more closely to the classic 'office' tradition, but need not be restrictive, and have a rich provision of seasonal resources.

- *Night Prayer* derives from the form of prayer which ended the monastic day, and is a simple pattern to complete the day.

Out of these patterns it is possible to derive a host of ways of praying. The intention was to provide resources which encourage diversity, whilst retaining, and extending to new contexts and people, a sense of shared prayer and praise.

Which office should I use?

The rest of this book will explore these orders in more detail. This quick guide will direct you to the chapters which will apply to your particular concerns.

If you are looking for a simple pattern of prayer, or one which will include regular prayer and Bible study, go to *Chapter 2: Using Prayer During the Day*.

If you want advice on how to use a more elaborate form of prayer, either once or twice per day, go to *Chapter 3: Morning and Evening Prayer*.

If you would like to add prayer at the end of the day to the rest of your prayers, or to use prayer at the end of the day as a simple form of daily prayer, then go to *Chapter 4: Night Prayer*.

Rhythms of prayer

The Bishop of Salisbury's Foreword to *Common Worship: Daily Prayer* says that the 'daily praying tradition of the Church of England . . . ranges more widely than the Daily Office'. One pattern of prayer does not fit all and, indeed, probably fits no one perfectly. The trick is to find your own rhythm, one which does not simply indulge your desires but properly meets your needs. The many resources in *Common Worship: Daily Prayer* are designed to help each worshipper and each worshipping community to join, in the words of the Foreword, 'in this living and developing tradition of daily prayer'.

I have served in two separate parishes which had previously had no tradition of saying the Office in church. When I advertised weekday Morning Prayer in the notice sheet for the first time I had no idea whether anyone would turn up, but knew that the possibility would at least get me out of bed. From that moment, in both situations, I was never alone as I prayed. And time after time people who joined me said the same thing: 'Why has the Church kept daily prayer a secret?' As they encountered it in a classic form in the offices of Morning and Evening Prayer, they were then able to adapt it so that they could find a discipline which would take account of their lifestyles and keep them connected with the corporate prayer of the Church. *Common Worship: Daily Prayer* will have succeeded if it allows daily prayer to go beyond the clergy (who 'have' to pray) and to nourish and enrich the lives of all God's people.

There is an exciting opportunity here to form people in the ways of prayer, and ways of prayer in the people. What follows in this book is not the authoritative description of 'how to do' *Common Worship: Daily Prayer*, but an opening up of the possibilities contained in its pages. Praise, prayer and Scripture are the essential elements, and in any combination and in any situation they can be none other than life-changing and life-forming, for they are to do with encounter with the living God.

2 Using Prayer During the Day

Jeremy Fletcher

Nothing quite like Prayer During the Day has been seen in the official prayer books of the Church of England before. It is intended to be a resource for daily prayer which is both easy to use and infinitely flexible. For many people Prayer During the Day may be the first step towards adopting a structured pattern of prayer, hence its position at the beginning of *Common Worship: Daily Prayer*. This new pattern of prayer has been designed to meet three different needs in the daily prayer of the Church.

- It provides a framework for personal *Bible reading* which nevertheless remains connected to the wider community of prayer.

- It restores a form of daytime or *midday prayer*, to be used in addition to the keystones of Morning and Evening Prayer.

- It responds to the pressures of modern life by providing a flexible pattern of prayer for a *single order* which can be used at any time of the day and made to fit any period of time.

Before we look at the many ways of using Prayer During the Day, it will be worth spending a little time exploring its background, and the different traditions of prayer which it is intended to serve.

Three sources of Prayer During the Day

Bible reading

Ordered reading of the Bible has always played a part in patterns of daily prayer. What has differed down the centuries and across the traditions is the way the reading from the Bible was chosen. On the one hand there is a *sequential* scheme. This makes sure that the Bible is read in a comprehensive pattern, and uses readings in sequence. Cranmer's preface to the first *Book of Common Prayer* in 1549 introduced such a yearly pattern, so that 'the people (by daily hearing of holy Scripture read in the Church) might continually profit more and more in the knowledge of God, and be the more inflamed with the love of his true religion'. A *thematic* scheme, on the other hand, chooses Bible readings which relate to the time of day, the day of the week, or the season of the Church's year, and has remembrance and proclamation as its prime purpose, not sequential reading of the Bible. Clearly both of these schemes are devotional, but they order the reading of the Bible in a different way.

Over time the reading and study of the Bible was to become an act of devotion in its own right, either instead of, or in addition to, the Daily Office. Many people found that detailed engagement with Scripture was made difficult by the long readings used at Morning and Evening Prayer, so alternative schemes were devised for personal devotion. One significant development came with the Evangelical Revival of the eighteenth century. The study of Scripture became a bedrock of personal devotion, and since then many have followed William Wilberforce's pattern of early rising, prayer and Bible study, though not many would berate themselves, as he did, for only having half an hour, rather than his usual two hours.

Primarily a feature of evangelical spirituality, the Quiet Time came to be seen as a mainstay of evangelical spiritual life. In more recent years the Quiet Time has been resourced by Bible reading notes supplied by different agencies, primarily as an aid to individual study but also as a way of creating a community of Bible readers; not for nothing is one of the agencies called the Scripture Union. Though there has been a general encouragement to offer praise and prayer as part of the Quiet Time, none of the commercially produced notes offer material for worship or intercession, and this has led to the separation of the corporate action of the Daily Office from personal Bible reading and study.

A related tradition of Bible reading is that reflected in the Roman Catholic Church's Office of Readings. The Second Vatican

Council (1962–5) restored the reading of Scripture to a primary place in public worship and, amongst other things, commissioned the three-year lectionary for Mass, which is the basis of the *Common Worship* principal service lectionary. The Council also took steps to re-shape the number of offices required for a pattern of daily prayer. It kept Lauds and Vespers as the key points of Morning and Evening Prayer, and reduced the other offices to three: midday prayer (the Little Hour) and Night Prayer (Compline), together with Matins, which was to be an Office of Readings with the study of Scripture at its heart. The Office of Readings can be used at any time during the day.

Prayer During the Day has been conceived in response to this ancient and contemporary desire to read the Bible both as a form of learning and also devotionally within the context of prayer. It gives the Quiet Time a clear structure and provides a wide diet of intercession and praise. Not only will this help those looking for a pattern for their devotional Bible study, it will also connect the personal devotion of individuals to the corporate prayer of the Church, which is the great strength of the Office of Readings in the Roman Catholic tradition. In no way does Prayer During the Day restrict how you choose to read the Bible, and those familiar with the Quiet Time tradition or that of the Office of Readings will find themselves at home in these pages.

Midday Prayer

The whole business of praying at set points during the day echoes the monastic pattern of prayer, established from the fifth century onwards. Prayer took place at seven points during the day and made use of eight offices. Lauds and Matins together were the early morning office, followed by Prime, Terce, Sext, None, Vespers and Compline. The monastic pattern was reviewed regularly over the next thousand years and took on a wide variety of local forms. It was not until the Second Vatican Council in the 1960s that the Roman Catholic Church initiated a thoroughgoing reform of the breviary (or pattern of daily prayer) which resulted, as we have seen, in a basic pattern of Morning Prayer (Lauds) and Evening Prayer (Vespers), together with Midday Prayer and Night Prayer (Compline), supplemented by a 'free floating' Office of Readings based on Matins.

In the Church of England thoroughgoing reform took place much earlier. In 1549 Cranmer introduced just two offices:

- Morning Prayer, derived from Matins, Lauds and Prime; and

- Evening Prayer, derived from Vespers and Compline.

Cranmer did not make use of the offices of Terce, Sext and None, which took place during the day. In recent decades, however, there has been increasing pressure among Anglicans for some form of set prayer during the day. The Roman Catholic Church provided this with the Little Hour of Midday Prayer. Other Anglican Provinces provided a simple form of Midday Prayer when they revised their prayer books[1] and *Celebrating Common Prayer* went a step further in offering a form of Midday Prayer which varied with each day and season. As befits a book which derived from a religious community, Midday Prayer in *Celebrating Common Prayer* makes obvious use of the traditional features of the monastic daytime offices, especially the use of Psalm 119, a hymn, and the opening versicle and response ('O God make speed to save us/O Lord make haste to help us').

In response to this felt need for a simple office in addition to Morning and Evening Prayer, Prayer During the Day provides a framework for Midday Prayer without restricting this kind of 'daytime' prayer to midday alone. It uses the key aspects of the monastic daytime offices (the versicle and response and the regular reading of Psalm 119), and could easily be adapted to form the basis of Terce, Sext and None for those who want to follow all the monastic hours. Daytime prayer in the monastic tradition tended to make use of shorter readings from Scripture, and these are duly provided in Prayer During the Day for occasions when it is used as a Midday Office rather than a structure for the extended study of the Bible.

Prayer During the Day provides a creative opportunity to follow in the monastic tradition, but to adapt it to contemporary life. You are not tied in to a restrictive timetable but given a framework within which to develop a pattern of prayer in the day which can be shaped around many different lifestyles.

A single order

For all of its history, daily prayer in the Church of England has been focused on two offices, one in the morning and one in the evening. This emphasis is reflected both in the requirement for clergy to say the two offices, and for the parish priest to provide them for the public on a daily basis in the parish church. Not everybody is able to follow this pattern, and the use of one office of praise, prayer and Bible reading has become increasingly popular. Those praying in this way have found that the orders for Morning and Evening Prayer have been inflexible and best suited to a church context; they have not translated well into prayer at home or before work, for example. However, people have valued the sense that in saying the Office they are connected to the prayer offered by the universal Church.

Prayer During the Day is a response to this need for a simple form of office for use once a day. It provides an adaptable framework which contains the three essentials of daily prayer:

- praise

- intercession

- Bible reading

At the same time it is also expandable in a number of different ways. As a framework, it encourages users to develop their own pattern of prayer while also connecting them to the wider prayer of the Church. If you are praying just one office a day, Prayer During the Day may well be the place to start.

Features of Prayer During the Day

As with every form of service in *Common Worship*, Prayer During the Day begins with a description of its structure, which is as follows:

Structure

¶ **Preparation**
A versicle and response, or a verse from the Psalms, or another introduction. A Form of Penitence may be used here or in the Prayers.

¶ **Praise**
An acclamation, hymn, song, or other act of praise

¶ **The Word of God**
A psalm, and one or more Bible readings

¶ **Response**
A versicle and response, or less formal response

¶ **Prayers**
Intercession, a Collect and the Lord's Prayer

¶ **The Conclusion**
A closing prayer, dismissal, blessing, or other ending

Each aspect of Prayer During the Day can be made as simple or elaborate as the local or personal situation demands. As with other services in *Common Worship*, the forms provided in the book are simply outworkings of the basic structure, not the only way to do it.

The Notes provide more detail about putting Prayer During the Day into practice. This depends very much on the particular way in which Prayer During the Day is going to be used, of which more below, but there are some general principles which can be elaborated as we begin.

1 Preparation

The Preparation may include a versicle and response or a personal prayer for the inspiration of God's Spirit. 'O God, make speed to save us. **O Lord, make haste to help us**' is especially appropriate when Prayer During the Day is being used as an office in addition to Morning, Evening and Night Prayer.

In monastic times, participants were encouraged to prepare in private for the daytime offices, and this time would culminate in the versicle and response asking for God's help. The Quiet Time tradition has emphasized the role of the Holy Spirit as the supreme interpreter of Scripture, and has always encouraged people to pray for the Spirit's help at the beginning of Bible study. Prayer During the Day offers two alternatives: the traditional monastic versicle and response, and a verse from the Psalms which either asks for God's help or focuses on the God who comes to those who call. This example is from Prayer During the Day on Wednesday:

Preparation

O God, make speed to save us.
All **O Lord, make haste to help us.**

(or)

Make me to know your ways, O Lord,
And teach me your paths.   *Psalm 25.3*

Preparation could clearly involve further texts, silence, or some symbolic action, depending on your context. An individual preparing for Bible study might want to make use of the Prayer before Bible Reading on p. 353 in the resource section.

---

2 Praise

Praise may include a song, hymn or scriptural song, or take the form of a time of corporate singing or extempore praise. *Hymns for Prayer and Praise*, the *New English Hymnal* and other collections contain 'office hymns' which may be used here.

No texts are printed for this section of Prayer During the Day, because there is such a wide variety of forms of praise that people will find appropriate. So the following is printed in the text of Prayer During the Day:

Praise

A hymn, song, canticle or extempore praise

The note refers to some of the possibilities here, many of which boil down to taste. It also mentions the 'office hymn'. The term refers to hymns reflecting the time of day and the season of the Church's year, specially written for the ancient monastic hours of prayer. These office hymns did not make it into *The Book of Common Prayer* but, like many aspects of daily prayer, continued to be used or were rediscovered during the nineteenth century. Collections such as *The English Hymnal* (1906) brought them into popular consciousness and inspired the writing of new hymns as well as the translation of existing Latin texts. *Hymns for Prayer and Praise*[2] is the most recent and comprehensive collection. If Prayer During the Day is being used in the tradition of the monastic daytime offices, as Midday Prayer or as Terce, Sext or None, then the use of one of these hymns would be more than appropriate.

Other possibilities include the use of canticles and scriptural songs, many of which are found in the resource section of *Common Worship: Daily Prayer*, or further hymns, songs, or spoken acts of praise. In a group setting this could also include an extended act of sung praise. Though thanksgiving is essential in the life of worship, it is worthwhile making the distinction between *praise* for who God is and *thanksgiving* for what God has done. All too often times of open or extempore praise take the form of thanksgiving for what God has done for us and end up focusing more on the worshippers than on God himself. Open times of praise will benefit from a steer from the worship leader to focus on the attributes of God at this stage.

The next section of Prayer During the Day is *The Word of God*. Again there is very little printed in the text:

The Word of God

A psalm, and one or more Bible readings

The Notes divide this into two elements: Psalmody and Readings.

> **3 Psalmody**
> At least one psalm should be included on each occasion.
>   Two tables making use of Psalm 119 (the great psalm of contemplation on God's word) and Psalms 121–131, 133 (the Psalms of Ascent, used by pilgrims on the way up to Jerusalem) on a weekly, fortnightly and monthly pattern are provided. These are especially appropriate when Prayer During the Day is being used alongside the other offices.
>   The psalm marked for 'Daily Prayer' or 'Single Office' in the *Common Worship* Weekday Lectionary will be appropriate if Prayer During the Day is being used as the only time of prayer in a day. Alternatively, any section of Psalm 119 may be chosen.

This note is very permissive, and it is worth spending some time looking at what it encourages you to do. Much depends on the context in which Prayer During the Day is being used, and especially whether Prayer During the Day is the only time of prayer on that day.

Midday office: using Psalm 119

Use the table of Psalms provided in the text (p. 34), based around Psalm 119. This psalm was a feature of the monastic offices – so much so that Cranmer complained that it was 'daily said and oft repeated' whereas other psalms were never used at all. Its use is appropriate here, however, not only because it is traditional, but also because it is indeed 'the great psalm of contemplation on God's word', as the note puts it. When Psalm 119 occurs in the lectionary provision for Morning or Evening Prayer, an alternative is always provided for the sake of those who will be using it at Midday Prayer.[3] Life would be much easier if there were 28 or 31 sections of this, the longest psalm, because it could then be used in neat sections in a monthly pattern. Unfortunately there are only 22. As a result, Prayer During the Day offers four solutions:

- 22 days of the individual sections of Psalm 119, the remaining 9 days using the Psalms of Ascent (Psalms 121–131 and 133)

- 14 days using longer portions of Psalm 119 for seven days and the Psalms of Ascent for seven days

- 7 days just using the longer portions of Psalm 119

- Choosing any section of Psalm 119 you like!

Midday office: using other psalms

You are not restricted to using Psalm 119 and the Psalms of Ascent at Midday Prayer. For instance, you could choose to use the psalm provided by the Weekday Lectionary for 'Daily Prayer'. However, you would need to note that this psalm is sometimes also used as the psalm for Morning or Evening Prayer.

Single order

If Prayer During the Day is being used as the sole daily act of prayer and praise then a wide choice of psalms is open to you. The *Common Worship* Weekday Lectionary provides a single psalm for Daily Prayer, or you can take your pick from any of the psalms provided for Morning and Evening Prayer that day, as well as from Prayer During the Day's own psalm table.

---

4 Readings

One of the following is used:

¶ The short reading printed in the order – especially when Prayer During the Day is being used with Morning and Evening Prayer.

¶ On weekdays one or more of the readings appointed in the *Common Worship* Weekday Lectionary.

¶ The readings in the column marked 'First Office' will unite users of a single office or quiet time with the praying of those who use Morning and Evening Prayer.

¶ The readings in the column marked 'Second Office' are a series of self-contained passages, well-suited to the needs of those new to Bible reading or who are making occasional use of Bible readings.

¶ The readings in the column marked 'Holy Communion' will suit those who on some days go

---

to Holy Communion and on other days wish to
maintain the continuity of readings.
¶ On Sundays and Principal Holy Days one or both of
the readings appointed for the Third Service are used if
not used at another service that day.
Personal or corporate Bible study might also take
place at this point.

What type of reading you choose depends on whether Prayer
During the Day is the only act of prayer on a particular day, or is
taking its place amongst a number of offices. A later chapter will
explore the *Common Worship* Weekday Lectionary as a whole,
so here we will look at its specific application to Prayer During
the Day.

Prayer During the Day as a Bible study

If you are using Prayer During the Day as a framework with
Bible reading as its centre, you still need to decide on a pattern of
readings. You may well choose to follow the lectionary readings,
using a commentary or even a devotional book to stimulate
further reflection. Whatever route you select, it is essential to
plan ahead by deciding which of the chosen readings will be the
focus for detailed study. Each lectionary has its own rationale,
discussed in more detail in a later chapter. Another option is to
adopt a pattern of readings chosen by one of the Bible reading
agencies. These have the added benefit of providing notes to
enhance understanding of the text. This latter option is not
mentioned in the Notes, but is clearly within the scope of Prayer
During the Day, especially if another office is being used with
readings from one of the lectionaries.

Prayer During the Day as an office

Will Prayer During the Day be the only office you use for the
day? If so, choosing a reading or readings from one of the
lectionaries makes perfect sense, as this will unite you with others
across the Church who are also joining in daily prayer. If Prayer
During the Day is being used in addition to Morning and/or
Evening Prayer, then an option would be to use one of the

lectionaries in the morning and/or evening and the short readings provided in the text at Prayer During the Day. Alternatively, the short readings could be used in the morning or evening and the longer lectionary readings at Prayer During the Day. The main point here is that at Prayer During the Day you use either a long or short reading, but not both! The short readings provide a limited diet and make no claim to be comprehensive, but they give an idea of how particular portions of the Bible can focus the theme of a day or season. They can act both as a short proclamation and also as the basis of an extended meditation. Longer and more discursive readings might not lend themselves to that treatment. Twenty-eight readings are provided for 'ordinary weekdays' (four per day for four weeks) and a reading per day is provided for seasonal time (seven readings, Sunday to Saturday for each season).

After the Word comes the next major section, the *Response*. The text given is again from Prayer During the Day on Wednesday.

Response

Silence, study, song, or words from Scripture, such as

The love of Christ compels us.
All **We are ambassadors for him.**

The note is equally short and permissive!

---

5 Response
A versicle and response are provided for use after the reading. Other appropriate responses include silence, group discussion, responsive prayer and singing.

It is not for a rubric, a note, or even a book like this to try to dictate how the individual may wish to respond to an encounter with God in the reading of the Bible. However, any proper reading or hearing of the word of God will, by definition, provoke a response. This may entail action, repentance, thanksgiving, further reflection, praise or even bewilderment. Simply to say 'amen' and move on is to circumscribe the possibility of God effecting change in us, and at the very least a short period of *silence* is in order. The 'responsory' grew up in the monastic tradition of daily prayer. It provides a spur to further reflection by placing a classic verse from Scripture up against the passage which has been read and allowing the two to resonate with one another. A short example of this is given in Prayer During the Day for each day and season, and longer patterns are found in the orders for Morning, Evening and Night Prayer.

Many praying groups have found that a short *discussion* in response to the reading has opened up new insights. Individuals have also found the use of a prayer journal helpful here, and writing a *prayer* in response, or even speaking one spontaneously can be an effective way of planting a new insight into the heart as well as the mind. Spoken and *sung praise*, perhaps majoring more on thanksgiving as the response of a changed heart to God, are also possibilities here.

Of course, one obvious response to God's word is prayer. This takes us into the next major section of Prayer During the Day, the *Prayers*. The example given is again from Prayer During the Day on Wednesday.

Prayers

Prayers may include these concerns

¶   *All who follow Christ, for growth in discipleship*
¶   *All in the medical profession*
¶   *All who have no one to pray for them*

Forms of prayer can be found on pages 330–356.

The Collect of the day or the following prayer is said.

Reveal in us your glory, Lord;
    stir in us your power.
Renew in us your kingdom, Lord;
    strengthen in us your hope.
Work in us your miracles, Lord;
    abide in us yourself.   *Daily Prayer (Diocese of Durham)*

The Lord's Prayer is said.

The note says this:

> ### 6 Prayers
>
> The Prayers may include a litany, open prayer, or a pattern of intercessions. Forms of intercession are provided on pages 330–356. This section should also include the Lord's Prayer and the prayer provided in the text, the Collect of the day, or some other prayer.

For each day of the week and each season of the year Prayer During the Day suggests three broad topics for the intercessions. These are printed in table form in the resource section of *Common Worship: Daily Prayer* (pp. 328–329), where you can get an idea of the breadth of subjects covered. Again, these are only optional suggestions, and it is also possible to make use of the fuller patterns of intercession in the resource section (pp. 330–345), as well as any other form of set prayer or open prayer.

The Lord's Prayer is included as a matter of course, though no text is included in the printed orders. This is to allow local usage to prevail, and any one of four versions of the Lord's Prayer may be used. Three of these are to be found on pp. 26–27 of *Common Worship: Daily Prayer*:

- 'Our Father in heaven . . .'

- 'Our Father, who art in heaven . . .'

- the 'ecumenical' contemporary version which has 'Save us from the time of trial' rather than 'Lead us not into temptation'

- 'Our Father, which art in heaven . . .' (the form in *The Book of Common Prayer*) is also legal but is not printed.

Just one other prayer is required: the Collect set for the day, or the prayer printed in the text, or what the note (p. 33) refers to as 'some other prayer'. Given that the description of the structure of Prayer During the Day speaks of 'a Collect' being used at this point, the 'other prayer' referred to in the note might naturally be in collect form, but the permission is intentionally wide. The prayers provided in the text have been chosen with two criteria in mind. Firstly, they are not used as collects anywhere else in *Common Worship* (apart from the Palm Sunday Prayer).

Secondly, they have formed part of the wider Christian praying tradition and would be included in most collections of prayers.

Like the short readings, this collection of 15 prayers makes no attempt to be comprehensive but is intended to act as a gateway to all the rich resources of Christian prayer down the ages. Other collects are to be found in the resource section, and the collects provided in the text of the orders of Morning and Evening Prayer can also be used.

Prayer During the Day ends with *The Conclusion*, as seen in Wednesday's example:

The Conclusion

May God who made both heaven and earth bless us.
All **Amen.**

The note says:

---

7 The Conclusion
The office concludes with a dismissal, a closing prayer, or another ending.

Prayer During the Day prints a short corporate blessing. Because this is in 'may God bless us' form, anyone can say it: you do not need a priest. Any form of ending is, however, appropriate. A praying group might well require some form of dismissal, or the Grace. An individual at Bible study might offer a prayer of commitment. As long as there is a clear signal that the office has ended, that is enough!

Prayer During the Day: weekdays and seasons

Common Worship: Daily Prayer prints an Order for Prayer During the Day for each weekday in 'Ordinary Time', and separate orders for eight seasons of the Church's year. This is a new way of doing things for those raised on *The Book of Common Prayer* and *The Alternative Service Book 1980*, which simply printed one order for Morning Prayer to be used on every day of the year. Those who have used *Celebrating Common Prayer* will be familiar with the introduction of a different order for each day of the week. CCP also gave each of those daily orders a distinctive 'seasonal feel' so that they could also be used as seasonal forms of service. So rather than print a separate order for Advent, for example, *Celebrating Common Prayer* gave Tuesdays an Advent feel and told you to use the Tuesday order on every day during Advent. This was very neat, but it did feel odd asking people on a December Friday to turn to the order for Tuesday and some users found it rather confusing. The Pocket Edition of CCP made things clearer by calling the offices 'Form 1, Form 2 . . .' rather than 'Sunday, Monday . . .' but each form still served both one day of the week *and* one of the seasons of the year.

Common Worship: Daily Prayer helpfully separates the weekdays of Ordinary Time from the orders to be used in seasons, so that in Advent you use the Advent order every day, and in Ordinary Time the relevant orders are used on each day of the week. All you have to know is whether you are in a season or in Ordinary Time, and what day of the week it is if you are in Ordinary Time. There is a very useful table on pages xiv and xv of *Common Worship: Daily Prayer* which defines when a season begins and ends. However, do bear in mind that Prayer During the Day is designed partly for those who are new to structured patterns, so it is probably best not to get too hung up on the rules and regulations about what should happen when.

Seasonal orders

Prayer During the Day provides the following seasonal orders (please note that the themes given here are not exhaustive, but provide an idea of the subject of prayers and readings printed in the text). It would be entirely appropriate to use one of these orders 'out of season' if the readings or theme for prayer on that day tied in with the theme of a seasonal order.

Season	Theme
Advent	The coming of the Word made flesh; the second coming; penitence and preparation; light and dark
Christmas	The Incarnation; Christ the light of the world
Epiphany	Revelation; the glory of God
Lent	Penitence and preparation for Easter
Passiontide	The suffering Christ; the suffering world
Easter	Resurrection; renewal and new life
Ascension to	The ascended Christ; waiting for the Holy Spirit
Pentecost	The gifts and fruit of the Spirit
All Saints	Any saint's day; All Saints' tide

Special features of the seasonal orders

Building on the structure of Prayer During the Day, certain features change for each season. These are:

- the verse from the Psalms in the Preparation

- the choice of short readings (one for each day of the week, so seven in all)

- the versicle and response in the Response section

- the theme of the Prayers

- the Collect provided

- the text at the Conclusion.

Weekdays in Ordinary Time

Sometimes praying the same thing every day can get boring. Ordinary Time lasts for roughly half the year and there is a large block of it between Pentecost and Advent. However, even ordinary days have had significance for Christians, and throughout the history of the Church certain weekdays have been associated with particular themes. Sunday is clearly the day of resurrection, the first day of the week, and Friday, the day of crucifixion, remains a day of penitence and fasting (or at least eating fish) for many. *Common Worship: Daily Prayer* does not force associations on other weekdays, but does make each day slightly different from the others. In both Prayer During the Day and Morning and Evening Prayer, 'flavours' which resonate with some of the traditional associations are given to each day. It is not worth making too much of this, but the flavours are as follows:

Sunday	Resurrection, heavenly hope
Monday	Holy Spirit, creation, the new life
Tuesday	The word of God, proclamation, communication
Wednesday	Discipleship, the kingdom of God
Thursday	Unity, reconciliation, Holy Communion, healing
Friday	Penitence, prayer, forgiveness
Saturday	Saints, the life of heaven

The way to spot the flavours is to look at the material which changes on each day, notably the short readings, the versicle and response in the response section, and the prayer at the end of the intercessions. Each ordinary weekday has four short readings, headed Week One, Week Two, and so on, so 28 readings are provided in all for Ordinary Time. With the 56 readings for seasons, the short readings form a useful collection of key Bible verses. This does not pretend to be exhaustive and other collections are available.[4] The only drawback with using other readings is that they may not tie in exactly with the other changeable material, especially in seasons, but this could be an opportunity to mine the Bible for your own key texts in order to broaden what is provided.

Using Prayer During the Day

Prayer During the Day is a simple and flexible resource for daily prayer which can be used in any number of ways. Once you have decided the purpose you want it to serve, many of the choices, which initially look a touch complicated, will fall into place. The Introduction outlines the possible choices:

¶ **Introduction**

Prayer During the Day provides material for a number of patterns of prayer.

¶ It provides a framework for a daily Quiet Time and Bible study – an Office of Readings.

¶ It is a single order for those who wish to be united with the Church's daily corporate offering of prayer.

¶ It is a simple order for use during the day, with Night Prayer as a simple evening office.

¶ It is Midday Prayer for those who wish to supplement the saying of Morning and Evening Prayer.

¶ It is a model for prayer at the third, sixth and ninth hours – traditionally called Terce, Sext and None – as used by some religious communities and their associates.

So what is it to be?

Bible Study
Ignore the short readings, choose a pattern of Bible readings to study, perhaps from one of the lectionaries. Use the verses suggested from Psalm 119.

Single Order
Ignore the short readings and choose one of the lectionaries to follow; perhaps use more material for prayer and praise, including a canticle, and perhaps the collect for the day. Use the psalm set for 'Daily Prayer' in the lectionary.

Simple Order
Use Prayer During the Day and Night Prayer as a twofold office, and decide how simple you would like this to be. Night Prayer also provides short readings: do you want short readings at each office, or a longer reading from one of the lectionaries? A canticle might be a useful addition. Use the psalms set for Morning and Evening in the lectionary.

Midday Prayer
Use the Psalm 119 table in one of its forms. Decide whether the longer lectionary readings are happening at Morning/Evening Prayer or at Midday Prayer.

Terce, Sext, None
You probably know what you require! Divide Psalm 119 into separate portions for each office. *Hymns for Prayer and Praise* has hymns for each of the hours, and the short readings can be divided up to suit. *Celebrating Common Prayer* includes prayers for Terce, Sext and None on pp. 270 and 271.

Individual or corporate?

The structure of Prayer During the Day is ideally suited for use by a group, either as a simple office, or as the structure of a group Bible study with prayer and worship.

Some churches and communities have fostered the idea of contemporary corporate prayer by providing all their members with a simple office and encouraging it to be used at a certain time of day, wherever people happen to be. The knowledge that others will be praying at that time, and that some of them might be in church, brings a community together spiritually even when it is separated geographically. Prayer During the Day would function excellently in this way, as its flexibility allows a local 'feel' to develop. Using specially written prayers would enhance this even further.

The structure of Prayer During the Day is also simple enough to be written on a bookmark, to be placed in a Bible, as the focus of a Quiet Time or period of Bible study. Here is an example which makes use of material from a number of orders of Prayer During the Day. It would be very simple to put the monthly pattern of Psalm 119 and the Psalms of Ascent on the reverse of the bookmark, or to have two orders for variety.

Prayer During the Day

Daily Bible Study

Preparation

Make me to know your ways, O Lord,
And teach me your paths. *Psalm 25.3*

Praise

Blessed be the God and Father of our
Lord Jesus Christ, who has blessed us
in Christ with every spiritual blessing
in the heavenly places. *Ephesians 1.3*

The Word of God

A Psalm

A Bible Reading

Response

May your word live in us

and bear much fruit to your glory.

Prayers

Reveal in us your glory, Lord;
   stir in us your power.
Renew in us your kingdom, Lord;
   strengthen in us your hope.
Work in us your miracles, Lord;
   abide in us yourself.

   Daily Prayer (Diocese of Durham)

The Lord's Prayer is said

The Conclusion

May Christ dwell in our hearts
through faith.
Amen.

---

3 Morning and Evening Prayer

Jeremy Fletcher

Prayer During the Day is *Common Worship: Daily Prayer* at its most flexible, allowing a simple structure to be used in a variety of ways and for a variety of purposes. Those used to the Church of England's inherited patterns of prayer will find the orders for Morning and Evening Prayer more familiar; these come after Prayer During the Day in *Common Worship: Daily Prayer*. As we have already seen, there have been different patterns of daily prayer, some elaborate and some simple, throughout the history of the Church. Even the simplest scheme has made room for prayer at the beginning and end of the day. In this sense, when Cranmer reduced eight monastic offices to two he was not simplifying a complex pattern of prayer but returning to a classic pattern of corporate prayer which had been established in the life of the Church as early as the third and fourth centuries.

Many of us have been shaped by *The Book of Common Prayer* and, more recently, *The Alternative Service Book 1980*. If this is the case for you, you will at once recognize the centrality of Morning and Evening Prayer in *Common Worship: Daily Prayer*, although the 'feel' of the material and some of the texts will be unfamiliar to you. If, on the other hand, you have been a regular user of *Celebrating Common Prayer*, you will feel very much at home with both the structure and the texts of *Common Worship: Daily Prayer*. You will also notice one major change: where *Celebrating Common Prayer* connected each day of the week with a season of the Church's year (so Wednesday was also the Christmas Season), in *Common Worship: Daily Prayer* the days of the week and the seasons of the Church's year have been deliberately de-coupled. Now there is an 'ordinary' Wednesday and a separate order for the Christmas Season.

A survival guide to Morning and Evening Prayer

You will do more than survive if you:

- are sure of the structure;
- learn to spot optional material;
- decide what options you are choosing;
- know what day of the week it is;
- remember your Bible and the psalm;
- decide how you are going to intercede.

Prayer During the Day is a very simple office which needs you to do quite a lot of work by inserting texts and making choices. Morning and Evening Prayer are actually more elaborate, but do all the work for you by printing fully worked-out orders for Morning and Evening Prayer with everything you need in the text, apart from the Psalm, the Bible reading and the Intercessions. You do not have to make any other choices if you do not want to. So:

Be sure of the structure

The essential elements of Morning and Evening Prayer are Praise, Scripture and Prayer. Morning and Evening Prayer in *Common Worship: Daily Prayer* handle these elements in a particular order, and the structure is shown in both a basic and expanded form.

Basic structure

    Preparation

    The Word of God

    Prayers

    Conclusion

This is the best structure to start with, because the full text of Morning and Evening Prayer can look quite confusing if you do not know where you are, especially when all the options are included or other permitted material is inserted. On the structure page below, the basic structure is flagged up by the type size and colour of the heading. In the orders of Morning and Evening Prayer these headings are in bold type at the right-hand side of the page. If you are printing your own version it is best to follow this principle and decide how you will signal this basic structure.

Expanded structure

Morning and Evening Prayer

Structure

Preparation

If desired, the Order may begin with one of the Forms of Penitence (pages 20–25) or, in the morning, The Acclamation of Christ at the Dawning of the Day (pages 82–83), or, in the evening, The Blessing of Light (pages 84–85).

The minister and the people call on the Lord to bless their worship as they offer prayer and praise.

The Word of God

The people of God listen and respond to the Word of God. This includes

¶ **psalmody**
¶ an **Old Testament Canticle** in the morning, if desired
   a **New Testament Canticle** in the evening, if desired
¶ **reading(s) from Holy Scripture**
¶ a **Responsory**, if desired
¶ a **Sermon** (here or before or after the Prayers) and
   a **Creed** or **Authorized Affirmation of Faith**, if desired
¶ the **Gospel Canticle: *Benedictus*** in the morning,
   Magnificat in the evening

Prayers

The minister leads the people of God in prayer. This includes

¶ **intercessions** and, especially in the evening, **thanksgivings**
¶ the **Collect of the day**, or some other Collect
¶ the **Lord's Prayer**

Conclusion

The service concludes with a **blessing** or other ending.

Now it gets more complicated, as the basic structure allows different types of material to be used, though always within the basic overall pattern. For example, the Preparation can include:

• Responses

• Glory to the Father (the Gloria Patri)

• A Prayer of Thanksgiving (Blessed are you . . .)

• An opening prayer

• A Form of Penitence

• The Acclamation of Christ at the Dawning of the Day (morning)

• The Blessing of Light (evening)

We will look below at what might influence these choices.

Learn to spot optional material

In the worked-out orders of Morning and Evening Prayer there are parts which are required and parts which are optional.[1] Optional texts are indented on the page, but this can be quite subtle on occasions, particularly when such material is at the top of a page and all you have to go on is a lot of white space to the left of the text.

The first note about Morning and Evening Prayer is very helpful here, because it spells out what material is required.

¶ Opening response
¶ Glory to the Father (or, in seasons, Prayer of Thanksgiving)

¶ Psalmody
¶ Reading
¶ Gospel Canticle

¶ Intercessions
¶ Collect
¶ Lord's Prayer

¶ Blessing

Here is how this required material fits into the basic structure:

Preparation

¶ Opening response
¶ Glory to the Father (or, in seasons, Prayer of Thanksgiving)

The Word of God

¶ Psalmody
¶ Reading
¶ Gospel Canticle

Prayers

¶ Intercessions
¶ Collect
¶ Lord's Prayer

Conclusion

¶ Blessing

The rubrics also indicate what material is optional by using the word 'may'. The rubrics for the Responsory ('a responsory . . . may follow'), and the Gloria after the psalm ('Each psalm or group of psalms may end with') make this clear and are followed by indented text. Other rubrics have to be more subtle, because they have to cover a number of eventualities, but the clue should be there somewhere.

Decide what options you are choosing

We shall look below at some of the reasoning behind the options, but the possible choices are listed here.

Optional texts included in the orders include:

- The Opening Canticle
- The Opening Prayer (Ordinary Time)
- The Prayer of Thanksgiving (seasonal time)
- The Gloria after the psalm or psalms
- The Old Testament Canticle (morning)
- The New Testament Canticle (evening)
- The Responsory
- Responses during the Intercessions
- Part of the Conclusion

Other options *within* the order include:

- The number and position of the readings
- Other hymns or canticles instead of those printed
- Use of silence at various points
- Use of set forms of prayer from the resources section
- A choice between the Collect of the day and the one printed in the service
- Different versions of the Lord's Prayer

Variations *to* the order include:

- Using The Acclamation of Christ at the Dawning of the Day instead of the Preparation at Morning Prayer.

- Using The Blessing of Light instead of the Preparation at Evening Prayer.

- Using one of the Thanksgivings (pp. 270–280) instead of the Prayers and Conclusion.

- Using Te Deum Laudamus – A Song of the Church, Gloria in Excelsis – A Song of God's Glory, or A General Thanksgiving immediately before the Conclusion.

- Using one of the Forms of Penitence (pp. 20–25) either instead of the Preparation, or within the Preparation after the Glory to the Father (Ordinary Time) or Prayer of Thanksgiving (seasonal time)

Know what day of the week it is

This may well be the hardest thing to remember first thing in the morning or last thing at night after a busy day. The serious point here is that orders for Morning and Evening Prayer come in two basic types:

- forms covering each day of the week in Ordinary Time; and

- appropriate forms for use every day during the seasons.

In seasonal time (Advent, Christmas, Epiphany and so on) you use the order for that season, every day of the week. In Ordinary Time (3 February to Shrove Tuesday and the day after Pentecost to 31 October) you use the order for the particular day of the week. On a Wednesday in Advent you use the order for Advent. On a Wednesday in Ordinary Time you use the order for Wednesday.

Remember your Bible

And choose your lectionary. The General Introduction to *Common Worship: Daily Prayer* opens up the possibilities here.

What to Read

Common Worship: Daily Prayer builds upon the flexibility allowed for in the Lectionary. The Lectionary (published separately), which will need to be at hand, provides two tracks of readings suitable for the office, each with an Old Testament and a New Testament reading. However, some will want to use Prayer During the Day as their opportunity for sustained engagement with Scripture and will concentrate their reading of Scripture there, thus freeing Morning or Evening Prayer to focus more on praise and intercession.

What pattern of Bible reading will you use? Up to now, the lectionary provided in the Church of England for Morning and Evening Prayer was made up of two longish readings in the morning and two in the evening, each reading following on from the previous morning or evening, so that there were four separate sequences of readings going on. Some people used these (or alternative) readings at other times of the day and had very short readings at the main offices.

Morning and Evening Prayer in *Common Worship: Daily Prayer* does not make any assumptions about the pattern of Bible reading to be used, and does not depend on any one pattern. The two main lectionaries, the Office and Second Office lectionaries, provide two readings each, and in that sense will be familiar to those who have used the Church of England's existing lectionary for Morning and Evening Prayer. The Second Office lectionary is governed by different principles, and these are discussed in Chapter 5, but apart from the fact that the readings are not necessarily sequential, the 'feel' of the readings is much the same as what has been available before. What is new is the encouragement to use short readings (such as those in the text of Prayer During the Day, or some other set) at Morning and Evening Prayer, and the suggestion that the Daily Holy Communion lectionary could also be used at Morning and Evening Prayer, especially if this would help those who are unable to attend a daily Eucharist on every occasion. As the General Introduction continues (p. ix):

> The important thing is to make responsible decisions about
> the use of Scripture that allow for reflection on God's word.

Bible reading at Morning and Evening Prayer:
choices to make and resources available

- *Two large readings at both Morning and Evening Prayer*

  Readings from *two* of the Office, Second Office or Holy
  Communion lectionaries.

- *Two large readings at a single office of either Morning or
  Evening Prayer*

  Two readings from *one* of the Office, Second Office or
  Holy Communion lectionaries.

- *One large reading at both Morning and Evening Prayer*

  Readings from *one* of the Office, Second Office or Holy
  Communion lectionaries, split over the two offices.

- *Short readings at Morning or Evening Prayer*

  Readings taken from the choice in Prayer During the Day,
  or some other collection. Longer readings used at another
  time during the day.

Remember the psalm

The *Common Worship* Weekday Lectionary makes specific and
clear the psalms to be used at Morning and Evening Prayer. If
only one office is used each day, however, a choice is necessary.
The most appropriate option might be either the Morning or the
Evening psalm (depending on the time of day) or, alternatively,
the psalm marked for daily prayer. The psalms for Morning and
Evening Prayer do not relate to the readings but have been
chosen for their appropriateness to, among other things, the time
of day. If the Holy Communion lectionary is being used as an
office lectionary, it might, therefore, still be appropriate to use the
Morning or Evening Prayer psalm, rather than the psalm set in
the Eucharistic lectionary.

Decide how you are going to intercede

Apart from the psalm and the Bible reading, the only text which is not printed in full in the orders for Morning and Evening Prayer is the intercession. Instead there is a rubric which looks like this:

[Morning]

Prayers

Intercessions are offered
¶ *for the day and its tasks*
¶ *for the world and its needs*
¶ *for the Church and her life*

These responses may be used

Lord in your mercy   *(or)* Lord hear us.
hear our prayer.   **Lord, graciously hear us.**

The cycle on page 328 and the prayers on pages 330–331 may be used.

Silence may be kept.

[Evening]

Prayers

Thanksgiving may be made for the day.

Intercessions are offered
¶ *for peace*
¶ *for individuals and their needs*

These responses may be used

Lord in your mercy   *(or)* Lord hear us.
hear our prayer.   **Lord, graciously hear us.**

The cycle on page 328 and the prayers on pages 332–333 may be used.

Silence may be kept.

Many forms of intercession are provided in the resource section on pp. 330–345, and intercession and thanksgiving may be made in any appropriate way. You simply need to be aware (preferably before you launch into Morning or Evening Prayer) how you are going to tackle this part of the office.

The Orders for Morning and Evening Prayer

Having survived, now is the time to look in a little more depth at the principles upon which Morning and Evening Prayer have been constructed.

Seasons and Ordinary Time

The structure of Morning and Evening Prayer is the same for Ordinary Time and seasons. Within the overall structure, however, there are some significant differences between the two.

Broadly speaking, the seasonal orders contain material which obviously relates to that season's themes, while the weekdays of Ordinary Time contain material which hints at a theme but does not make this very obvious. The seasonal themes used by Prayer During the Day (see p. 37 above) are also used for Morning and Evening Prayer. Similarly, the different flavours of weekdays in Prayer During the Day are also applied to Morning and Evening Prayer. A general difference between seasons and Ordinary Time is that in the Preparation in Ordinary Time the Gloria Patri ('Glory to the Father . . .') is used, whereas seasons have a prayer of thanksgiving. Otherwise the elements of the orders of Morning and Evening Prayer are the same: it is the choice of text which marks out the differences.

Variations

The following texts are different for each day of the week and for each season:

• Opening Canticle

- Old Testament Canticle (mornings) or New Testament Canticle (evenings)

- Responsory

- Refrain to the Gospel Canticle

- The Collect printed in the text

In addition, these texts are different for each season:

- Introduction to the Lord's Prayer

- The concluding prayer

Common Worship: Daily Prayer works on the basis that where Morning and Evening Prayer are concerned, it is more user-friendly to make the choices for you and print them out in a full text. This is preferable to providing a skeleton text and a large section of resources. However, the choices made in the printed forms are not designed to limit your scope. For instance, all the canticles are also printed separately in their own section, so it is possible to select other canticles if required. Alternative canticles are suggested in the text and a table of these alternatives is given on pp. 81–83 of Chapter 5 of this book.

Two entire pages of *Common Worship: Daily Prayer* (pp. xiv and xv) are devoted to telling you when each season starts and finishes. You do not have to be too slavish about this, and the sky will not fall in if you get bored with Epiphany after five weeks and use the ordinary weekday order instead. Indeed, it may well be that on a particular day in Ordinary Time either the Bible readings, a world or local event, or a particular theme for prayer mean that the penitence of Lent or the longing of Advent becomes appropriate, and there is nothing to stop you using these offices even if it is August.

The classic seasons of the Church's year are found here in a familiar and uncontroversial form but, like the *Common Worship* Sunday material, *Common Worship: Daily Prayer* also offers the possibility of using the period between All Saints' Day and the First Sunday of Advent as a time of 'celebration and reflection on the reign of Christ in heaven'. Though this is strictly Ordinary

Time, *Common Worship: Daily Prayer* provides a 'seasonal' order for Morning and Evening Prayer for this period. Some of the reasoning behind this 'Kingdom' season can be found in *The Promise of His Glory*,[2] which contains services and prayers from All Saints to the Presentation of Christ (Candlemas). The *Common Worship* Calendar keeps the Sunday before Advent as the Festival of Christ the King, and this theme fits well with other events of the late autumn, including Remembrance.

Canticles

One of the essential elements of Morning and Evening Prayer, along with Scripture and Intercession, is Praise. Traditionally this has taken the form of a canticle, a song of praise often derived from the Old or New Testament.[3] Three types of canticle are provided in Morning and Evening Prayer. In Ordinary Time, and in the morning office during seasonal time, the *Opening Canticle* is derived from a psalm and offers a further way of using the psalms in worship. Though the term is not used here, this opening canticle is sometimes referred to as the Invitatory. In seasons at Evening Prayer the Opening Canticle takes the form of a well-known hymn, to encourage the possibility of singing and provide a springboard for further praise in a variety of forms. A note says that the hymn printed is not the only one that can be used, and those using Evening Prayer in seasons are therefore encouraged to be creative.

At Morning Prayer, the canticle following the Psalm is an *Old Testament Canticle*, and at Evening Prayer it is a *New Testament Canticle*. In the history of daily prayer there have been different methods of choosing the canticles for each office,[4] though generally speaking the monastic morning office of Lauds used a canticle from the Old Testament. The *Common Worship: Daily Prayer* pattern can, therefore, claim some ancient precedent, though the specific provision of Old and New Testament Canticles for morning and evening respectively is only as recent as *Celebrating Common Prayer* for many Anglicans, and is a new feature of the Church of England's 'official' provision.

The first two canticles are optional and they vary from day to day and from season to season. By contrast, the *Gospel Canticle* is always the Benedictus (The Song of Zechariah) in the morning and the Magnificat (The Song of Mary) in the evening. Again, ancient precedents can be found for the use of these canticles at these times of day, but the use of two great songs from Luke as the invariable and required canticles is a new development in the Church of England. *The Book of Common Prayer* provided them, but with alternatives. *The Alternative Service Book 1980* placed them before the New Testament reading, in accordance with the view that they were 'pre-incarnational' because they were originally sung before the birth of Christ. *Common Worship: Daily Prayer* follows recent usage and makes them the point around which the office turns. The Gospel Canticle ends the Word of God section of the office with a confident response that God 'has come to his people and set them free' and 'has filled the hungry with good things'. The 'classic' Anglican canticles used at Morning and Evening Prayer like the Te Deum (A Song of the Church) and the Nunc dimittis (The Song of Simeon) can be found in *Common Worship: Daily Prayer*, but are moved elsewhere: the Nunc dimittis to Night Prayer, and the Te Deum to the resource section, with a note allowing its use at the end of Morning Prayer at any time.

The wide choice of Opening, Old and New Testament Canticles (there are over 70) will be familiar to users of *Celebrating Common Prayer*, but will be a fresh discovery for those who have used only *The Book of Common Prayer* or *The Alternative Service Book 1980*. The resources section prints all of them (pp. 493–573), starting with psalm canticles and then Old Testament, Apocryphal and New Testament canticles in biblical order. It is worth looking through all the texts to see the breadth and depth of what is provided. Thirty canticles are printed in the orders for Morning and Evening Prayer and the rest are offered as alternatives in the rubrics. It will take a long time to exhaust them all, though a decision has to be taken about whether you place more value on familiarity or variety.

Refrains

The use of refrains, also referred to elsewhere as antiphons, is another ancient feature of daily prayer which has now been restored to the Church of England in an official text. Often these were sung by the congregation, leaving a specialized musician to sing the words of the canticle or psalm. They often became quite elaborate in their own right and were taken either from the canticle itself, or from elsewhere in the Bible. In *Common Worship: Daily Prayer* the refrains for the canticles help to set the flavour of the offices in Ordinary Time and herald the theme of the offices in seasonal time. This can be seen most clearly in the refrains to the Gospel Canticles. In Ordinary Time the refrains come from the Benedictus and Magnificat themselves, whereas in seasons other portions of the Bible are used.

The most complex example of this is in Evening Prayer in Advent. A rubric on page 182 tells us 'From 17 December until 23 December, see page 362.' The text on page 362 is headed 'The Advent Refrains for the Magnificat (The Advent Antiphons)'. These ancient Advent antiphons have been used in the Church since the eighth century and are made up of different scriptural verses, each with a concluding prayer. They heighten the anticipation of the coming of Christ by drawing from the prophecies of the coming of the Messiah and the titles given to him in the Old Testament. Used in this way they resonate with the Gospel Canticle and focus the praise of the Church. The Advent refrains (sometimes called the 'Great O antiphons') are of such value that they have not only continued to be used, but also form the basis of the Advent hymn, 'O come, O come, Emmanuel'.

None of the other refrains are that complex, and they are all printed in the text rather than in a separate section, but many do have pedigrees just as ancient.

Collects

A collect is printed in each order for Morning and Evening Prayer. The collect is also an ancient feature of the prayer of the Church and has performed a number of functions in different contexts. In the Eucharist the collect was part of the Gathering, and was either a prayer for those who had collected to worship or, if there was a more elaborate introduction, collected together the praises of the people. In other types of worship, the intercessions were gathered together by a prayer in this form, and this is how it is used in *Common Worship: Daily Prayer*.[5] There is a long-standing tradition of making the collect set for Sunday the 'Collect of the week', and this was encouraged in *The Book of Common Prayer* and *The Alternative Service Book 1980* by the use of the Sunday collect and one or two others at the end of the office. *Common Worship: Daily Prayer* discourages the use of more than one collect, but leaves it open whether the collect used is the one set for the Sunday or one printed in the text. There is no 'preferred' choice.

The collects printed in the orders for Morning and Evening Prayer are again either part of the flavour of the weekdays of Ordinary Time, or more obviously part of the theme of the seasonal offices. Simple expediency and an immunity to page turning or ribbon insertion might dictate that the collect printed in the text is used, but *Common Worship: Daily Prayer* prints all the Collects for Sundays, Feasts, Holy Days, Festivals and Lesser Festivals. Further details about the collects can be found in Chapter 5.

Prayer of Thanksgiving

In seasons the Preparation at Morning and Evening Prayer includes a Prayer of Thanksgiving, always beginning 'Blessed are you'. These prayers are a familiar part of *Celebrating Common Prayer*, and *Common Worship: Daily Prayer* emphasizes their celebratory nature by making them a feature of seasons only, on the basis that you can have too much of a good thing. These prayers are a contemporary development based on ancient beginnings. In Jewish prayer the *Berakah*, or blessing prayer, was widely used, especially for God's provision of food and the gifts of creation, and formed the natural basis of eucharistic prayers in the Early Church. Such blessing prayers were also used for the blessing of light, or *Lucernarium*, where thanks were given for light to illuminate the darkness and for the light of Christ. The style of those prayers has been used for these more general thanksgivings, and their similarity to thanksgivings in the Eucharist is noticeable. Unlike the Eucharist, permission is given for them to be extemporized: Note 6 (p. 80) says it 'may be varied or improvised when appropriate'.

Other features of Morning and Evening Prayer

The following sections are all things in *Common Worship: Daily Prayer* which can be added on to, or replace, parts of the standard orders for Morning and Evening Prayer.

- The Acclamation of Christ at the Dawning of the Day
- The Blessing of Light
- Forms of Penitence
- Thanksgivings
- Prayers for the Unity of the Church
- Prayers at the Foot of the Cross
- A Commemoration of the Resurrection
- Vigil Office

The Acclamation of Christ and The Blessing of Light

Just in case the variety contained within the orders is not enough, *Common Worship: Daily Prayer* offers two more elaborate ways of beginning Morning and Evening Prayer respectively. The Acclamation of Christ (morning) and The Blessing of Light (evening) have ancient roots and replace the whole of the Preparation. *The Acclamation of Christ at the Dawning of the Day* includes verses from Venite – A Song of Triumph, which was traditionally used at Matins in the monastic pre-dawn office. The refrains are particularly appropriate for the dawn and seem less appropriate later. Two Prayers of Thanksgiving are printed and the rubric also allows one of the seasonal Prayers of Thanksgiving to be used.

The Blessing of Light derives from the ancient *Lucernarium*, or light blessing, which accompanied the lighting of the lamps. It also includes a Prayer of Thanksgiving, with rubrical permission to use a seasonal prayer, and verses from Psalm 141, the traditional evening psalm. Since this mentions incense, it may be appropriate to take the hint and burn some. It goes without saying that The Blessing of Light only makes sense if it is actually dark and a light is lit.

Forms of Penitence

Confession and Absolution only made their appearance in the Church of England's orders for Morning and Evening Prayer in 1552: Cranmer's original orders in 1549 began with 'O Lord open thou our lips', but the Reformation concentration on sin and forgiveness soon led to the inclusion of a daily act of public penitence. Though a form of penitence was a feature of Compline, there was little by way of penitence in the other monastic offices. Even now, *A Service of the Word* makes it essential to include confession and absolution only when Morning or Evening Prayer is used as the Principal Service on a Sunday. *Common Worship: Daily Prayer* includes four Forms of Penitence (pp. 19–23) which can be used if desired. Three of them have authorized prayers of confession and absolution and so conform to the requirements for an act of penitence in a Principal Service, and all can be used either as a penitential Preparation for Morning and Evening Prayer (especially appropriate in Advent and Lent) or as a part of the Preparation after the Glory to the Father or Prayer of Thanksgiving. The Notes (p. 19) suggest other penitential material that can be included and also remind you that Night Prayer and the Thanksgiving for the Word both include penitential material, so the Forms of Penitence are best omitted if one of these is being used that day.

Thanksgivings

Four thanksgivings are printed:

- Thanksgiving for the Word

- Thanksgiving for Holy Baptism

- Thanksgiving for the Healing Ministry of the Church

- Thanksgiving for the Mission of the Church

We have already seen that daily prayer in the life of the Church has been a mixture of praise, prayer and engagement with the Bible. These four thanksgivings provide the opportunity to focus on aspects of the life and mission of the Church, to give thanks for them and to offer prayers for them. No specific instructions are given for when they might be used, but it would clearly be appropriate to use the Healing Thanksgiving before and after a healing service, the Mission Thanksgiving around the time that link missionaries visit the church, the Baptism Thanksgiving at the time of baptism preparation, and so on.

The thanksgivings are exactly the same as those printed in the Main Volume of *Common Worship*, but their use in the office is more reflective than in a main service, and it may be that the element of intercession is more to the fore when they are used at daily prayer. In a main service, for example, testimonies can be given in the Thanksgiving for the Word, and prayer for healing take place during the Thanksgiving for Healing. At the office, prayers and thanksgivings might be made for those who will undertake these ministries in other places. When used at the office, the Thanksgivings replace the Prayers and the Conclusion.

Prayers for the Unity of the Church and Prayers at the Foot of the Cross

These two forms of prayer can also replace the Prayers and Conclusion at Morning and Evening Prayer. It has long been the practice of the Church to pray for unity, often on Thursdays, reflecting the prayer of Jesus in John 17 that his followers might be one, which he prayed on the night before he was crucified. A rubric suggests that a unity candle might be lit for this section (see Chapter 6 below). There may well be other symbols, often local, which will focus prayers for unity, and this prayer can take place at any time of day.

Meditation on the cross is also an ancient feature of daily prayer, particularly on Fridays and in penitential seasons. This form of prayer is also influenced by the Franciscans, as meditation on (and prostration before) the cross was a central part of the devotions of St Francis, and these prayers will be familiar to those who have used *Celebrating Common Prayer*. The rubrics encourage the use of a cross, with appropriate action and prayer.

A Commemoration of the Resurrection

The Commemoration of the Resurrection is really another form
of Morning Prayer for Sundays, but to be used in the very early
morning. It contains a full order for Morning Prayer, but with set
readings, canticles and psalms which focus specifically on the
resurrection. This order is particularly appropriate on Sundays in
Easter and might form the basis of a non-eucharistic dawn service
on Easter Day, if your church is unable to have an early Eucharist
at that time.

Vigil Office

Keeping a vigil in preparation for a major festival has long been a
tradition in some parts of the Church. The general pattern has
been to begin with a blessing of the light and acclamation,
continuing with a series of readings, each followed by a psalm or
canticle, a time of silence and a prayer, and ending with
intercessions. The Easter Vigil is the classic and most ancient
example, but there is ancient precedent for having a similar vigil
on the eve of other major festivals and even ordinary Sundays.
The Promise of His Glory gives examples of vigil services for
Advent, Christmas, Candlemas and Epiphany, for example, and
Common Worship: Daily Prayer provides a general outline of
such a vigil office, with the encouragement to adapt it as
appropriate.

The key elements are The Blessing of Light, a series of readings,
and the Gospel Reading and Collect for the next day. When used
as printed in *Common Worship: Daily Prayer*, the Vigil Office
conforms to the requirements of Evening Prayer. However, the
introductory rubric also gives the tantalizing suggestion that the
vigil could be kept less formally by the use of song, poetry and
testimony, and creative minds could develop all sorts of
celebrations out of this.

Other changes to Evening Prayer

Note 11 of the General Notes (p. xiii) hints at the traditional
practice of adapting Evening Prayer on the eve of Principal
Feasts. In practice this means that at Evening Prayer on the day

before a Principal Feast, texts specified for the Feast are used. Such material (sometimes called the 'propers') includes canticles, refrains and the collect. The Lectionary will also give readings for the eve of Principal Feasts. It is possible either to adapt Evening Prayer in this way, or to use the Vigil Office described above.

Note 11 indicates that on Saturdays and the day before a Principal Feast, Evening Prayer is always adapted in this way (unless the Saturday itself is a Principal Feast or Festival), but that local discretion can be used about doing the same for Festivals. So if you are celebrating the Lesser Festival that happens to be for your patron saint, you might well want to use the 'proper' material at Evening Prayer the night before.

This pattern of starting a celebration on the evening before derives partly from the Jewish practice of beginning the new day at nightfall, not dawn. One of the illogicalities of current Christian practice is that you can end up celebrating Evening Prayer for the feast twice: once the night before and once on the day itself. Any excuse for a party.

4 Night Prayer
Jeremy Fletcher

A brief history of Night Prayer

Compline was one of the ancient monastic hours of prayer. Its name derives from the Latin *completorium*, completion, and Compline brought the day to a close and was directly followed by sleep. It often took place as darkness fell, sometimes as early as 5.00 p.m. in the days of candlelight. It was a service which allowed participants both to reflect on the past day with thanksgiving and penitence, and to ask for God's protection through the vulnerable hours of darkness. Cranmer used aspects of Compline for his service of Evening Prayer, notably the Nunc dimittis ('Now, Lord, you let your servant go in peace' from Luke 2.29-32) and the collect against all perils which begins 'Lighten our darkness'.

As with the other monastic services which did not make it into *The Book of Common Prayer*, versions of Compline continued to be used 'unofficially'. A version appeared in the 1928 Prayer Book and, with some changes, this appears in the *Common Worship* Main Volume as 'Night Prayer in Traditional Language'. A modern language version called 'Night Prayer' appeared in *Lent, Holy Week, Easter* in 1984, and from this came Night Prayer in *Celebrating Common Prayer* and 'An Order for Night Prayer (Compline)' in the Main Volume. *Common Worship: Daily Prayer* makes no changes to the version in the Main Volume, but does provide extra resources for days of the week and seasons.

Structure

The structure page for Night Prayer reveals a simple fourfold shape, much like Prayer During the Day, but with a much more focused purpose and 'feel'.

Night Prayer (Compline)

Structure

Preparation

The minister **asks a blessing** on the life of all God's holy people.

Authorized Prayers of Penitence may be used.

A **hymn** may be sung.

The Word of God

This includes
¶ **psalmody**
¶ a **short reading from Holy Scripture**
¶ a **responsory**, committing oneself into the hands of God
¶ the **Gospel Canticle**: ***Nunc dimittis***

Prayers

Intercessions and thanksgivings may be offered.

The Collect is said.

The Lord's Prayer may be said.

The Conclusion

The service concludes with
¶ **a calling on God for protection** through the coming night
¶ a simple **blessing**

Using Night Prayer

The introduction to Night Prayer envisages that it might be used in church or at home. While it assumes a corporate context, Night Prayer can clearly also be used by an individual.

Understanding the key features of the service will help you to adapt it to your circumstances.

Night Prayer is a service of *completion*, and the service should genuinely end the day. The Introduction (p. 300) says:

> If there is an address, or business to be done, it should come first. If the service is in church, those present depart in silence; if at home, they go quietly to bed.

Night Prayer is a service of *quietness and reflection.* The atmosphere should be set beforehand and if possible an order of service should be provided which does not require obtrusive instructions. Any music should be reflective rather than boisterous. People should be given a good opportunity to reflect on the day that has passed. It is worth devoting time to planning how this will be introduced.

Night Prayer is an opportunity for *penitence.* Reflection on what has happened in the day will generally feature regrets as well as joys. Ending the day asking for God's forgiveness has been a feature of Compline from its earliest days, though this is not an essential part of Night Prayer. The notes make clear that the Prayers of Penitence may be omitted, and that this should be the case if such prayers have already been used that evening in another service.

Night Prayer is also an opportunity for *thanksgiving.* As people reflect on the past day they can be gently led to focus on thanksgiving. This may happen first during the opening period of reflection, which can move into thanksgiving rather than, or as well as, penitence. Secondly, in the Prayers both Intercessions and Thanksgivings may be offered. Texts are provided, but it may well be that an open time of thanksgiving is most suitable.

Night Prayer is about *commitment* into the hands of God and *protection* from evil. The onset of darkness may no longer be a time of fear for everyone, but the equation both of darkness with evil and of sleep with death remains. Night Prayer displays a sure confidence in the God who is a sure defence and the resurrection and the life.

Choices to make

The basic pattern of Night Prayer is very simple, and the initial order printed in *Common Worship: Daily Prayer* can be used on every day of the year. However, even with this simple order there are certain choices to be made, and it is also possible to vary the material with other texts printed in the pages which follow Night Prayer.

Initial choices

Penitence
If prayers of penitence have already been used that evening, it is appropriate to omit this section and begin with 'O God, make speed to save us'.

There is a prayer of confession printed in the text, but others can be used. Authorized confessions can be found on pp. 123–132 of the *Common Worship* Main Volume.

Thanksgiving
Will there be thanksgiving at the beginning or during the Intercessions? The General Thanksgiving can be found in the resource section of *Common Worship: Daily Prayer* (p. 355), or any suitable thanksgiving prayer may be used.

Hymn
The Latin hymn traditionally used at Compline was 'Te lucis ante terminum', and a translation is printed in the text (other translations are available). There are other appropriate hymns: *Hymns for Prayer and Praise* has a selection, and the 'Evening' section in other hymnals will contain hymns that reflect the particular concerns of Night Prayer.

Psalm
Psalms 4, 91 and 134 are printed in full, each of which has an association with evening and nightfall. Only one need be used.

Scripture reading
Three very short readings are printed. The purpose of a
Scripture reading in Night Prayer is to act as a focus for
prayer and reflection, rather than as a proclamation or as
the basis for an expository sermon. Only one of these
readings (or some other reading) need be used. The Notes
suggest that the Gospel Reading for the following day (if it is
a Sunday or a major festival) might also be an appropriate
choice, either before Night Prayer or in place of the set
reading.

Responsory
Alleluias may be added between Easter Day and Pentecost.

Prayers
No intercessions or thanksgivings are printed, so you will
have to decide what form to use. Many forms of intercession
can be found in the resource section of *Common Worship:
Daily Prayer*, but these are not the only possibilities.

A Collect ('Visit this place . . .') is printed, but others may be
used. Generally speaking the 'Collect for the Day' is less
appropriate than one which reflects the themes of Night
Prayer. A selection is offered in the pages which follow Night
Prayer.

Conclusion
The final versicle and response is only appropriate if Holy
Communion is the first service the next morning.

Daily and seasonal choices

Night Prayer at its heart is a simple office designed to bring the
busy-ness of the day to a close and also to welcome rest and
sleep. This is not the time for great variety or radical
experimentation. Nevertheless, a little seasonal variation is
possible. Rather than print separate orders for each weekday and
season, the writers and compilers of *Common Worship: Daily
Prayer* took the decision to print a single order of Night Prayer.

Only a few texts change for each weekday or each season, and some pre-planning will enable you to incorporate these whilst retaining Night Prayer's distinctive simplicity. The Notes also make it clear that variety is by no means compulsory and that the same order of Night Prayer can be used every day of the year. Here are the texts that can vary.

- *Daily*   An alternative psalm, short reading and collect are provided.

- *Seasonal* An alternative psalm, short reading, refrain for the Nunc dimittis, collect and blessing are provided.

The simplicity of Night Prayer will be enhanced by the printing of a separate order of service if at all possible. When books are being used, two markers will be required if the optional material is being used. One marker will be required for the psalm (because the text is only given by reference) and another one for the prayers and readings. Ideally, markers should already be in place in the leader's and congregation's copies before the service begins.

Night Prayer and Evening Prayer

We have already referred to the fact that Cranmer merged many of the monastic offices into just two orders of service. For Evening Prayer in *The Book of Common Prayer*, he borrowed the Nunc dimittis and 'Lighten our darkness' from Compline. Both of these have, of course, become indispensable features of Evensong for Anglicans. *The Alternative Service Book 1980* continued their use, and the unconscious connection of these two great texts with Evening Prayer will cause many people to be taken by surprise when using *Common Worship: Daily Prayer*. The tradition of daily prayer down the ages has been to have one 'Gospel Canticle' at Morning and Evening Prayer, so Cranmer rather complicated things by including both Magnificat and Nunc dimittis in Evening Prayer. *Common Worship: Daily Prayer* has restored the single Gospel Canticle to Morning and Evening Prayer, and so Nunc dimittis only appears in Night Prayer.

However, 'Lighten our darkness' has become such a feature of Evening Prayer that it was impossible to leave it out of the evening orders entirely. It appears both on Sundays in *Common Worship: Daily Prayer* and as an Evening Collect in the *Common*

Worship Main Volume. However, it has very much 'end of day' themes, so permission is given to use it 'on any day throughout the year' at Night Prayer. All you need to do is take care that if you have used Evening Prayer on a Sunday in Ordinary Time you are not repeating yourself – though with such a seminal prayer that may not be such a bad thing anyway.

Time, place and symbolism

As we have already seen, the monastic day ended early by modern standards, so Compline marked the onset of darkness rather than the end of a contemporary evening. The timing of Night Prayer is therefore up to local choice, but it should always mark the end of the day as a symbolic act of completion. Contemporary religious communities use it to mark the end of community life for the day and the point when they retire to individual rooms. Many churches use Night Prayer at the end of a central meeting or Lent study, and it works just as well at the end of an Alpha, Emmaus or confirmation course. In these latter cases it may well be good to have coffee and chat before Night Prayer rather than after. Individuals, couples or households can use Compline before retiring for the night.

Night Prayer is an intimate service, designed to serve the needs of worshippers, not the other way round. You do not have to pretend to be a monk to use Night Prayer, and you do not have to go into church to make it work. Nevertheless, there will be many people who encounter Night Prayer for the first time in a church setting. If a church decides to use Night Prayer, it might be wise to make it as simple and unchurchy as possible, to show how it could be used at home. After all, monastic communities describe themselves as families, and Compline completes the day in the monastic house. This is a time when the connection between a church celebration and prayer at home should be very clear.

Any visual aids or ritual movements need careful thought and should reflect the inherent simplicity of the office. Candles have traditionally been a feature of evening prayer. When the lamps were lit, it was inevitable that thoughts would turn to Jesus the light who shines in the darkness. However, that does not preclude using candles at Night Prayer also. Extinguishing the candles takes on a symbolic meaning as participants sense the need for God to watch over us during the hours of darkness. Other symbols (such as an evening newspaper to symbolize the events of the day) could be used as aids to reflection and meditation, providing this is done discreetly.

Night Prayer and Prayer During the Day

The General Introduction to *Common Worship: Daily Prayer* suggests that some might want to use Prayer During the Day and Night Prayer as a simple twofold pattern of daily prayer, as an alternative to the more elaborate provision of Morning and Evening Prayer. Both Night Prayer and Prayer During the Day have simple structures and can be easily adapted, though Night Prayer has much more of a late evening feel and may need to be adapted for use at an earlier time of day. If you want to use Prayer During the Day and Night Prayer as a twofold office you will need to decide what to do about Bible readings and psalmody, since each of these offices provide only short readings. However, this may well be how those new to structured daily prayer can begin to pray more than once a day – by using two simple offices. If, as part of this pattern of praying, you wish to include a regular time of examination, reflection and thanksgiving at the end of a day, Night Prayer simply cannot be beaten.

5 Using the resource sections

Jeremy Fletcher

Introduction

If you compare the offices contained in *Common Worship: Daily Prayer* with those printed in *The Alternative Service Book 1980*, the difference is striking. In *Common Worship: Daily Prayer* each day of the week and each season has its specific prayers, canticles and responses, giving a rich variety of texts within a common structure. The ASB had one order to be repeated time after time, with little daily or seasonal variety. The rich resources of *Common Worship: Daily Prayer* cannot be contained within the pages of the offices themselves, however. There are separate resource sections full of forms of intercession, alternative canticles and the like, which can be used to give further variety and flavour to Morning and Evening Prayer, Prayer During the Day and Night Prayer. In this chapter we will look at these in some detail and explore ways in which the additional material could be used.

The first thing to make clear, however, is that, apart from the psalms, you don't actually *need* to use any of these additional resources at all. *Common Worship* has established a general principle that the amount of page turning should be kept to a minimum, and the orders for Morning and Evening Prayer contain everything you need for the office except intercessions, the Bible readings and psalms. You might well decide that there is enough variety in the orders as they are printed. But explore just a little beyond the beaten track and you will find that over half of *Common Worship: Daily Prayer* is given over to further resources which can be used to enrich the offices. Some texts are only applicable on specific occasions, and other parts of services (for example the intercessions) need to be left open for local practice, so a large section of resources is inevitable.

There are five sections of additional material, contained at the beginning and end of the book.

Introduction

A General Introduction, Notes, and the *Common Worship* Calendar, Forms of Penitence, The Lord's Prayer, The Apostles' Creed.

Prayers

Biddings, sample responses, a Cycle of Intercession, worked-out forms of intercession, litanies and other prayers.

Collects and Refrains

All the *Common Worship* Collects, including those for Lesser Festivals (which were not printed in the Main Volume of *Common Worship*).

Canticles

Every canticle referred to in *Common Worship*, including Psalm Canticles, Old Testament and Apocrypha, New Testament and Gospel Canticles, and some non-biblical canticles which are an ancient part of the Church's tradition (such as the Gloria in Excelsis).

The Psalter

The *Common Worship* Psalter is printed, but with additional material. The main difference from the Main Volume of *Common Worship* is that refrains are suggested and each psalm is provided with a psalm collect, a prayer based on the theme of the psalm.

Prayers

Intercession has been integral to patterns of daily prayer since the earliest days of the Church. From the fourth century, when the community gathered at the beginning and end of the day, the main activities were praise (using particular psalms) and prayers of intercession. Bible readings were not a feature of these gatherings: other services in the week were used for preaching and instruction. In later years this 'cathedral' or 'city' tradition of praise and prayer merged with the 'monastic' or 'desert' tradition of long Bible readings together with recitation of all the psalms on a regular pattern.[1] The result is that services of daily prayer nowadays seem to have been overwhelmed with both long readings *and* elaborate intercessions, and the temptation (as with the Evensong I have just attended) is to skimp on the intercessions. *Common Worship: Daily Prayer* gives freedom at this point, and it is worth planning what importance you will give to intercessions well before the service begins.

None of the orders for the offices of *Common Worship: Daily Prayer* give any texts for the Prayers. The rubric in each order is slightly different, however.

[Prayer During the Day, Wednesday]

Prayers may include these concerns:

¶ *All who follow Christ, for growth in discipleship*
¶ *All in the medical profession*
¶ *All who have no one to pray for them*

[Morning Prayer]

Intercessions are offered

¶ *for the day and its tasks*
¶ *for the world and its needs*
¶ *for the Church and her life*

[Evening Prayer]

Thanksgiving may be made for the day.

Intercessions are offered

¶ *for peace*
¶ *for individuals and their needs*

[Night Prayer]

Intercessions and thanksgivings may be offered here.

These rubrics are deliberately permissive, though they give a gentle steer towards thanksgiving in the evening. Prayer During the Day and Morning Prayer are seen as places for wide-ranging intercession, and Evening Prayer focuses more on individuals and the theme of peace.

The main decision to make in using the resources contained in the Prayers section is whether intercession or Bible reading and study will be the main focus of the office. This decision should be agreed upon before the office begins, to give time for preparation. If intercession is to play the prominent part, it is worth delving into the rich variety of material on offer in these pages.

Starting from its opening page, where 4 possible opening sentences and 19 different responses are provided, the resource section offers a whole host of possibilities. Nine of these responses are appropriate for 'seasonal' use (e.g. 'Risen Lord: hear our prayer') but, due to their obvious versatility, they are not given a seasonal heading. This is another point at which some pre-planning is vital, since the forms of intercession come with a symbol showing the place for a response, but do not give a text. It is just conceivable that someone might use the Christmas intercessions (e.g. 'Wonderful Counsellor, give your wisdom to the rulers of the nations') with this seasonal response: 'Lord, we come to the cross: in your mercy hear us', but common sense will generally prevail. Wise leaders of intercessions give the words of the response and then practise it immediately with the congregation if it is not printed in a service sheet. This is a good habit to adopt. Some biddings go on for a long time before the first response happens, and people's memories are short.

Prayer During the Day suggests three different broad topics for prayer per day, and these are printed in full as A Cycle of Intercession on p. 328 of *Common Worship: Daily Prayer*. Extempore intercessions, where an individual or members of a group pray out loud without any formal preparation, can be very powerful, but often focus narrowly on local and repetitive concerns. In response to this problem, this cycle of intercession covers a wide range of themes which, if used as the basis for extempore prayer, will ensure that intercession is neither repetitive nor insular. It reflects the 'flavour' of each weekday and the theme of each season. Epiphany, for example, suggests prayers for unity, peace and healing. Friday has prayers for courage to take up the cross, the right use of authority, and for victims and perpetrators of violence. If a group is using Prayer During the Day, or these themes are being used at Morning, Evening or Night Prayer, why not nominate someone to lead the intercessions and give them access to these themes before the office begins to help them give structure to their prayers.

Twenty-one forms of intercession are provided, from a variety of sources. They take the form of short biddings (brief sentences which open up a theme for prayer) and indicate a place for a response. Two are specific to mornings, one to evenings and one to the late evening, and the rest are 'suitable for seasonal use'. You are encouraged to use them flexibly, and here again a little preparation will immeasurably enrich the experience of intercession, as the following examples show.

Silence between the biddings is both simple and effective but, especially in groups, it is tempting to make the silence very short. As the leader, count to ten as a minimum, and then begin to think about the next bidding. Thirty seconds or a minute is even better: use a watch.

The theme of each section could be introduced, followed by *open prayer*, then the bidding could be used to close each section. Clear instructions to help people pray out loud are vital. If you really want people to pray out loud, avoid the temptation to say 'Let us pray either out loud, or in the silence of our hearts'! The silence of our hearts is much more comfortable and always wins in this situation. It is always easier for people to speak out names or short phrases, so begin with these, giving the subject for prayer clearly.

A *group prayer time* could begin with individuals sharing their concerns, followed by a time of silent or open prayer, and finally a set form of intercession. This closing intercession might well be one of the Litanies, numbers 21–26 in the Prayers section. Drawn from the psalms, these litanies are, in essence, general prayers which could themselves act as structures for intercession. However, they work best when used as a whole, as simple versicles and responses. In this case, everyone will need the words in front of them and some instructions as to how they will be used. Any practical notice like this is best done before the intercessions start, even before the service, if possible.

The use of litanies has a long history in the life of the Church, and the term can nowadays refer generally to prayers in which a series of biddings are interspersed with a fixed congregational response. There is also a more 'fixed' set of prayers in this pattern, known in the Church of England, since *The Book of Common Prayer*, simply as The Litany, and its *Common Worship* version is provided here. The Litany in full is a long prayer, but it is possible to use only certain sections, always beginning with the first and concluding with the last. It is frequently customized in this way for a particular occasion (as happens in the Ordination Service, for example), and as a long-standing part of the tradition of the Church of England it is right that it takes its place here. Alternatively, it would not be stretching things too much to pray the Litany over a week, use one section per day, or linger over particular sections, perhaps even including visual pointers to prayer at appropriate points (see Chapter 6, 'Beyond words', for lots of ideas along these lines).

A small section of 'Other Prayers' includes

- A Prayer Before Bible Reading

- Collects for Morning and Evening

- A New Year Collect

- A contemporary form of the General Thanksgiving

- An Indian prayer for protection before sleep, called the Christaraksha

- The Kaddish, a Prayer of a Jewish Mourner which is usable as a song of praise far beyond the context of a funeral

- A Dismissal Prayer.

Collects and Refrains

At a quick glance you might think that this 140-page section just reprints the collects from the Main Volume, but here, as with the psalms, *Common Worship: Daily Prayer* gives added value. *Common Worship* introduced a new set of collects, first published in 1997 in *Calendar, Lectionary and Collects*. The Main Volume only included the collects for Sundays, Principal Holy Days and Festivals. *Common Worship: Daily Prayer* provides all the collects because, along with Sundays, Principal Holy Days and Festivals, it also needs the collects for Lesser Festivals, the Common of the Saints and Special Occasions.

The collect is a characteristically brief form of prayer which obeys clear rules in its construction. Traditionally it has brought to an end or 'collected' a time of silent or open prayer, and in the Eucharist it functions as the hinge point between the Gathering and the Liturgy of the Word. The Collect for the Sunday, because it was used through the week at Morning and Evening Prayer from Cranmer's time on, also became a sort of 'prayer for the week'. Recent Church of England history has fluctuated in this regard, however. *The Alternative Service Book 1980* gave every Sunday a theme, and the collect was often so closely related to this and the Sunday readings that it was quite difficult to use for the rest of the week when separated from those thematic readings. The *Common Worship* collects are not related to specific readings and are therefore more generally usable throughout the week and as the gathering together of a time of prayer.

Which collect is used?

Prayer During the Day, Morning, Evening and Night Prayer all bring the time of intercession to a close by using a collect. Only Night Prayer restricts the choice of collect (you can use either 'Visit this place' or 'Lighten our darkness'). The other orders suggest the Collect of the Day, and also print a general prayer (in Prayer During the Day) or collect (in Morning and Evening Prayer) as an alternative. There is a tradition that Saturday Evening Prayer makes use of the collect from the following Sunday. The same can happen at Evening Prayer on a weekday before a Festival, though the note on page xiii says that the collect is only used if the readings for that Festival are also used.

The *Collect of the Day* is the collect set for the previous Sunday, unless the day is a Principal Feast or Holy Day (bold and red in the Calendar), in which case it will have its own special collect. (Some communities use the collect of a Principal Feast or Holy Day at Evening Prayer on the day before as well, just to confuse things.)

If the day is a Festival (red, not bold, in the Calendar), a Lesser Festival (black) or Commemoration (*italics*) then you can choose either the special collect or the collect from the previous Sunday.

If in doubt, the alternative collect printed in the text is always available. You are advised by the notes that 'normally' only one collect is used on any occasion.

Refrains

Special introductions and endings to the Gospel Canticles have traditionally been used at Morning and Evening Prayer as a way of marking out seasons and festivals.[2] These refrains are provided in the text of Morning and Evening Prayer for each of the weekdays and seasons. Refrains for other occasions are provided separately in this part of the resource section. Each refrain needs to be placed before and after the canticle to which it is assigned and the worshippers alerted to the change, ideally by having a special order of service printed, or their attention drawn to the special refrain before the office begins. Two refrains are given for the Magnificat: one for use at Evening Prayer *before* the Festival, and one for use at Evening Prayer on the day itself. This again might be confusing unless it has been made clear beforehand which one is to be used.

Canticles

Common Worship: Daily Prayer contains 79 canticles. The word canticle simply means 'little song', and almost all of them are given the title 'song' (e.g. 'A Song of Christ the Servant'). With a few exceptions, these canticles are all drawn from the Old and New Testaments or the Apocrypha. Using scriptural material in this way again hails from the earliest days of the Church.

Originally the term canticle described any scriptural song that was not a psalm. However, the definition soon widened to include newly written songs which were generally accepted by the Church. Eventually canticles came to include songs formed from selected verses from psalms, or indeed whole psalms such as Psalm 95 (Venite – a Song of Triumph) and Psalm 100 (Jubilate – a Song of Joy). As theological disputes overtook the Early Church, non-scriptural songs were avoided, because they might be theologically 'unsound', so only a small number survived. The three most ancient in *Common Worship* are Phos Hilaron – a Song of the Light; Te Deum Laudamus – a Song of the Church; and Gloria in Excelsis – a Song of God's Glory. To these have been added A Song of St Anselm, A Song of Julian of Norwich and, the most recent, Saviour of the World.

The orders for Morning and Evening Prayer all contain three canticles:

- an opening canticle, taken from a psalm

- a canticle from the Old Testament (in the morning) or the New Testament (in the evening)

- a Gospel Canticle.

Of these, only the Gospel Canticle is mandatory. Alternative Old and New Testament Canticles are suggested at all times, with more alternatives suggested during seasons because the seasonal order is used every day and in a long season some variety is welcome. You are encouraged to use alternatives and your initial choice is a guided one, but these suggestions are just that, suggestions, and different canticles may be appropriate in more than one season. For example, the canticles suggested for Lent may well be appropriate during Advent if the theme of the office is based more around penitence than around the traditional pre-Christmas theme of preparation.

A handy guide to the alternatives

Here in table form is a guide to the Canticles and their alternatives suggested in the daily and seasonal orders of Morning and Evening Prayer.

Weekdays	Canticle	Alternative(s)
Sunday Morning	Song of David (21)	Song of the New Creation (30) Bless the Lord (47)
Sunday Evening	Song of the Lamb (69)	Song of Redemption (59) Song of the Heavenly City (71)
Monday Morning	Song of Deliverance (26)	Song of Ezekiel (38)
Monday Evening	Song of God's Grace (57)	Song of God's Children (55)
Tuesday Morning	Song of Peace (23)	Song of God's Chosen One (25)
Tuesday Evening	Song of the Holy City (70)	Song of the Lamb (69)
Wednesday Morning	Song of the Word of the Lord (31)	Song of the Lord's Anointed (33)
Wednesday Evening	Song of the Blessed (50)	Song of Praise (66)
Thursday Morning	Song of the Covenant (29)	Song of Tobit (41)
Thursday Evening	Great and Wonderful (68)	Song of Christ's Appearing (60)
Friday Morning	Song of Humility (39)	Song of the Word of the Lord (31)
Friday Evening	Song of the Justified (54)	Song of Christ's Glory (58)
Saturday Morning	Song of Jerusalem (36)	Song of Pilgrimage (45)
Saturday Evening	Song of God's Love (65)	Song of the Blessed (50)

Seasons	Canticle	Alternative(s)
Advent Morning	Song of the Wilderness (27)	Song of God's Herald (28) Song of Baruch (46)
Advent Evening	Song of the Spirit (72)	Song of the Justified (54) Song of the Lamb (69)
Christmas Morning	Song of the Messiah (24)	Song of Hannah (20) Song of God's Chosen One (25)
Christmas Evening	Song of Redemption (59)	Song of God's Love (65) Song of the Holy City (70)
Epiphany Morning	Song of New Jerusalem (32)	Song of the Covenant (29) Song of the Bride (34)
Epiphany Evening	Song of Praise (66)	Song of Christ's Appearing (66) Great and Wonderful (68)
Lent Morning	Song of Manasseh (49)	Song of the Word of the Lord (31) Song of Humility (39)
Lent Evening	Song of Christ the Servant (63)	Song of Christ's Glory (58) Song of Repentance (64)
Passiontide Morning	Song of the Lord's Steadfast Love (35)	Song of Solomon (22) Song of Jonah (40)
Passiontide Evening	Song of Christ's Glory (58)	Song of Christ the Servant (63) Song of the Spirit (72)

Seasons	Canticle	Alternative(s)
Easter Morning	Song of Moses and Miriam (19)	Song of Solomon (22) Song of the New Creation (30)
Easter Evening	Song of Faith (62)	Song of God's Grace (57) Song of the Heavenly City (71)
Ascension/ Pentecost Morning	Song of Ezekiel (38)	Song of Judith (42)
Ascension/ Pentecost Evening	Song of God's Children (55)	Song of God's Grace (57) Song of Christ's Appearing (60)
All Saints/ Advent Morning	Song of the New Creation (30)	Song of the Righteous (43) Song of Wisdom (44)
All Saints/ Advent Evening	Song of God's Assembled (61)	Great and Wonderful (68) Song of the Holy City (70)

All the canticles in the resource section are used, or suggested for use, in the orders for Morning and Evening Prayer, whether as opening canticles, or as Old or New Testament Canticles. In the course of a year, this means that someone using the orders to their fullest extent will enjoy a rich diet of over 70 songs of praise from the Scriptures and the writings of the Early Church. However, the choices offered are not obligatory, and many of these canticles may be suitable on other days or in other seasons: some are already used more than once through the year. So it pays to become familiar with all the canticles and allow them to become part of the rhythm of prayer; a particular canticle might then suggest itself on a particular day, even though the book does not tell you to use it.

Using the canticles

Sing them

Above all, these are acts of praise and, long though the tradition
has lasted in the Church of England, saying them reverentially by
rote may not be the most worshipful way to use what are, after
all, songs! Various publishers, notably the RSCM and Kevin
Mayhew, have brought out music in different styles to
accompany Morning and Evening Prayer in the Main Volume,
and will do the same no doubt for *Common Worship: Daily
Prayer*. Though it may seem 'purer' to use the actual words of
the canticle in full with a specially composed musical setting,
metrical paraphrases of the best known canticles are also
plentiful, and an encouragement (or at least permission) for their
use is given in the General Notes.

Sing something else

Canticles found in the liturgy itself are clearly not the only way
of praising God in song. *Common Worship: Daily Prayer* drops a
subtle hint about this by using hymns instead of canticles in the
opening canticle slot in the seasonal orders for Evening Prayer, as
follows:

Advent:	Creator of the stars of night
Christmas:	Of the Father's love begotten
Epiphany:	O worship the Lord in the beauty of holiness
Lent:	Lord Jesus, think on me
Passiontide:	The royal banners forward go
Easter:	Ye choirs of new Jerusalem
Ascension:	Creator Spirit, Lord of Grace
All Saints:	Give me the wings of faith to rise

If you are annoyed by this choice and can instantly think of
better hymns, then you are doing exactly what was intended. The
texts are there to inspire other appropriate choices, not to restrict
what you can do. Use the seasonal indexes in hymn and song

books and choose hymns and songs which people can use as vehicles of praise.

In fact, you are not restricted to choosing a hymn only in a season. The General Notes say that any of the canticles may be replaced by suitable hymns and songs. This gives a real opportunity to find a means of expressing praise not only with singing, which is always better than simply reciting, but also by using a musical style which is truly expressive of a local situation. Some hymn-books will give you hymn versions of the better known canticles (e.g. 'Tell out, my soul' for the Magnificat), but you can get creative by delving into the scriptural indexes in the back of many hymn and songbooks to see if there are hymns and songs based on the Bible verses used in the canticles. It is more important that genuine praise happens than that people are squeezed into something which is perceived to be 'proper'.

Say them creatively

Traditionally people stand for the canticles, as for a hymn, and they are recited by everyone together. However, you can use the refrain, said by all, to punctuate sets of verses said by individuals, or verses could be said by different 'sides' of the congregation. You can also experiment with posture and movement: some of the penitential canticles (for example number 37, A Song of Lamentation) might best be said kneeling, and others contain hints about posture and gestures: 'Come, let us worship and bow down, let us kneel' (Venite – A Song of Triumph); 'Lift up your hands . . . and bless the Lord' (A Song of Worship).

Even if you do not sing, background music could be used while canticles are recited; and a symbol or picture could be used as a visual focus. The field is wide open for creative adaptation here: why not use the music from *2001, A Space Odyssey* (*Also sprach Zarathustra* by Richard Strauss) and a picture of the earth from space for Benedicite – A Song of Creation; or sand, water and a flowering plant with music from Haydn's *Creation* for A Song of the Wilderness. In short, do anything to lift the canticles beyond the mundane.

Psalms

The regular use of psalms in worship predates the Christian Church and was a tradition that Jesus and his disciples themselves inherited (e.g. Matthew 26.30). In the earliest days of the Church many psalms were perceived to be written prophetically about Jesus himself. For this reason the monastic tradition placed the reciting of all the psalms at the centre of its pattern of daily prayer. The choice of psalms for each day will be examined later in this chapter. Here we will look at the Psalter provided by *Common Worship: Daily Prayer*, and in particular features which have been provided in addition to the text of the psalms themselves.

Common Worship: Daily Prayer uses the *Common Worship* Psalter, which seeks both to maintain the connection with the praying tradition of the Church of England and to be accurate in its translation of the original Hebrew. The Coverdale psalms in *The Book of Common Prayer* are the 'root' of this tradition and a careful analysis of the text will reveal hundreds of phrases familiar to the English Church for half a millennium – the Coverdale psalms used in *The Book of Common Prayer* of 1662 predate that book by over a century. The *Common Worship* translation is contemporary to the extent that it is in 'you' form, it has been changed where Coverdale was inaccurate, and it has been made inclusive, where possible, of both men and women.[3] This is not the only translation of the psalms which is permitted for use in *Common Worship*; a note explains that any translation can be used 'which is not prohibited'. As yet, none is!

Added features

Though the translation of the psalms is the same, there are two main differences from the Psalter in the *Common Worship* Main Volume:

- A refrain is provided for each psalm, together with a symbol (℟) indicating where it can be used.

- A short prayer, called a Psalm Collect, is provided at the end of each psalm.

A typical psalm therefore looks like this:

Psalm 70

Refrain: Rise up, O Lord, and deliver me, O my God.

1 O God, make speed to save me; ◆
   O Lord, make haste to help me.

2 Let those who seek my life
        be put to shame and confusion; ◆
   let them be turned back and disgraced
        who wish me evil.

3 Let those who mock and deride me ◆
   turn back because of their shame. ℟

4 But let all who seek you rejoice and be glad in you; ◆
   let those who love your salvation say always,
        'Great is the Lord!'

5 As for me, I am poor and needy; ◆
   come to me quickly, O God.

6 You are my help and my deliverer; ◆
   O Lord, do not delay. ℟

                O God, our helper and defender,
                deliver us in our weakness,
                answer our longings
                and vindicate our faith,
                that we may see your glory
                in Jesus Christ our Lord.

Refrains

Refrains originated as a verse sung by the whole assembly, while only the cantor had the full text. For practical purposes this meant that only one text was required, which was helpful in the days before mass-produced copies. It also meant that in the days before musical notation, when all melodies had to be learnt by heart, the whole assembly could join in with a simple repeated tune and the skilled musician was left to handle the rest. Today that role is performed by responsorial psalms, in which a refrain is used in between the verses of the psalm. This is no new invention, and the creative hint was probably taken from the psalms themselves. Many psalms contain their own built-in refrains: Psalms 42/3, 67, 107, 136 are good examples.

The provision of refrains is simply designed to enrich the experience of those who pray the psalms. *Common Worship: Daily Prayer* in no way *requires* them to be used, nor does it imply that this is a better way of praying the psalms. However, the growth of such responsorial use of the psalms has been great, and the provision of refrains will allow the psalms to be prayed and sung in a number of ways, as appropriate to the local context. In *Common Worship: Daily Prayer* all the refrains are verses from the psalms, most of them taken from within the particular psalm. Some refrains have been chosen from other psalms – and again these are only suggestions: there may well be verses from other biblical books which would make equally suitable refrains.

The symbol (R) shows where the refrain is to be used in each psalm. The position of the refrain relates to those natural division points in the psalm which do not disrupt or distort its meaning. This means that there is no common pattern for all 150 psalms: the refrain does not come after every second verse, for example. Even within a particular psalm it is not always possible to have a regular pattern for placing the refrain. Psalm 5, for example, has refrains after 4, 3, 4 and 3 verses, and Psalm 10 after 7, 6 and 6 verses. This causes no problems when the psalm is said, but is more interesting when the psalm is sung, since most methods of singing the psalms require a regular pattern.

Remember that it is not necessary to use the refrains at all, and you can always use the refrain only at the beginning and end of the psalm. One common approach is for the service leader to say (or sing) the refrain and the congregation to repeat it. The service leader then reads the verses of the psalm, and indicates (either through tone of voice or a pause) when the congregation are to join in with the refrain. In this way only the service leader needs the text of the psalm. Again, clear instructions either before the office or before the psalm is said or sung will help worshippers relax into praying the psalms, rather than worrying about what is going to happen next.

Psalm Collects

The other valuable feature of the Psalter in *Common Worship: Daily Prayer* is the prayer, called a Psalm Collect, which is printed at the end of each psalm (and at the end of every three sections of Psalm 119). This idea will be familiar to users of *Celebrating Common Prayer*, but may be new to many approaching this sort of material for the first time.

Psalm Collects originated in the monastic tradition as meditative prayers to punctuate the saying of the psalms and respond to their themes. The psalms were seen to resonate with the life of Jesus Christ and it was important to highlight this, using specially composed prayers. These collects also served to 'christianize' the psalms, and functioned in much the same way as the Gloria Patri ('Glory to the Father', said or sung at the end of the psalm) has done in the tradition of the Church.

The Psalm Collects in *Common Worship: Daily Prayer* come from a variety of sources. The majority were originally written by the authors of *Celebrating Common Prayer*. Around a third of the Psalm Collects are new compositions by members of the Liturgical Commission's Daily Office Group. I was fortunate to be one of the authors and can testify to the way that composing a prayer out of an engagement with a psalm opens it up to new and surprising meanings. I would encourage you not only to use the prayers provided, but also to try and write your own. It can change your relationship with the psalm and certainly makes you pray it with heightened awareness.

Enthusiastic as I am about the Psalm Collects, they are there to serve, not to be served. They can be used instead of, or in addition to, the Gloria Patri, they can be prayed silently, or used as the basis for extempore prayer in response to the psalm. If they distract from the psalm, simply do not use them. Like the refrains, they are optional, and throughout *Common Worship:*

Daily Prayer this optional material is signalled by being indented and in lighter type.

Choosing a psalm to use

The *Common Worship* Weekday Lectionary offers a number of ways of using the psalms. One column, the Psalmody column, offers psalms for both morning and evening, chosen to go with the time of day. It also offers a psalm which can be used if you are saying only one office in a day. Another psalm is provided if the Second Office lectionary is being used for a service of Holy Communion.

Be careful here. Some commercially produced lectionaries put the morning psalms with the Office Lectionary and the evening psalms with the Second Office Lectionary. This is fine if you are using the Office Lectionary for your morning readings and the Second Office Lectionary for the evenings, but can get confusing if you use the readings at different times: you have to remember to detach the psalms from the readings!

The Weekday Lectionary introduces a way of choosing the psalms which will be new to those who have not used *Celebrating Common Prayer*. Up to now the official lectionaries of the Church of England have followed the classic practice of using the psalms in sequence. Monastic communities in particular developed elaborate ways of praying all the psalms all of the time, and some cathedrals followed suit. More than one undertook to say all 150 psalms each day, which would only really leave time to eat and sleep! Anglicans inherited this pattern of praying all the psalms in sequence in the monthly cycle of psalms in *The Book of Common Prayer*, and later the seven-week cycle in *The Alternative Service Book 1980*.

The approach used by the writers and compilers of *Celebrating Common Prayer* was different. They followed another tradition, which selected psalms appropriate to the time of day or to the season of the Church's year. This approach means that in seasons the psalms chosen can resonate subtly with the themes and Bible readings. Psalm 22 ('My God, My God, why have you forsaken me?') is clearly relevant to Passiontide, for example, and Psalm 70, looking for God's deliverance, reflects the concerns of

Advent. This approach also guards against some clashes: Eastertide is a joyful season, but the practice of saying the psalms in sequence means that you can end up saying psalms of lament during most of it. The writers and compilers of *Common Worship: Daily Prayer* decided, therefore, to make use of both these patterns. The result is that in Ordinary Time (roughly the period between the Presentation of Christ and Ash Wednesday and between Pentecost and Advent) the psalms are read in sequence in the morning and evening lectionary, using all 150 psalms three times a year. In seasonal time, on the other hand, the psalms are chosen on a weekly pattern to reflect the concerns and themes of the season. This latter approach may seem confusing to those raised on the sequential pattern alone, but is worth persevering with. This confusion is compounded by the fact that the Lectionary begins with a seasonal selection in Advent, and the choices may make sense only after being used for a full year. More than one person has complained that the repeated use of certain psalms in seasons must have been a typesetting error!

Using the psalms

So you have decided which psalm to use, how you are going to deal with the refrain, and whether you will end with the Psalm Collect. Exhausting as this decision-making process may be, there is more to come. How will you *say* the psalm? A 'traditional' way of saying the psalms is to say either each half of a verse, or whole verses, 'antiphonally', that is, alternately. If you can, look carefully beforehand at the psalm you are going to use. Some psalms use parallelism, so that the second half of a verse says the same thing as the first, using different words. These psalms will benefit from being said antiphonally by half verses. Others will make sense when different voices say alternate verses, and others work best when groups of verses are said by an individual.

Where one group of people is saying a whole verse, the custom has emerged of leaving a short pause at the half way point, marked in *Common Worship: Daily Prayer* by the diamond sign (♦). If you are leading a group which includes newcomers or visitors, make sure you give clear instructions about this before you start. If you are joining in prayer with a new group yourself,

Lent 2

		Principal Service	3rd Service	2nd Service	Psalmody
Sunday	24 February P(La) 2nd Sunday of Lent	Genesis 12.1–4a Psalm 121 Romans 4.1–5, 13–17 John 3.1–17	Psalm 74 Jeremiah 22.1–9 Matthew 8.1–13	Psalm 135 [or 135.1–14] Numbers 21.4–9 Luke 14.27–33	DP 121

		Holy Communion	Office	2nd Office or Alt HC	Psalmody
Monday	25 February P(La)	Daniel 9.4–10 Psalm 79.8–9, 12, 14 Luke 6.36–38	Genesis 41.25–end 1 Corinthians 4.8–21	2 Kings 20.1–11 Luke 14.1–14 HC Ps 13	MP 26, 32 EP 102 DP 12
Tuesday	26 February P(La)	Isaiah 1.10, 16–20 Psalm 50.8, 16–end Matthew 23.1–12	Genesis 42.1–17 1 Corinthians 5.1–8	Isaiah 57.14–end Luke 14.15–24 HC Ps 32.9–end	MP 56 EP 38 DP 116
Wednesday	27 February P(La)w George Herbert, priest, poet (see p.66)	Jeremiah 18.18–20 Psalm 31.4–5, 14–18 Matthew 20.17–28	Genesis 42.18–28 1 Corinthians 5.9—6.8	Numbers 27.15–end Luke 14.25–end HC Ps 77.16–20	MP 3, 6 EP 90 DP 108
Thursday	28 February P(La)	Jeremiah 17.5–10 Psalm 1 Luke 16.19–end	Genesis 42.29–end 1 Corinthians 6.9–20	Joel 2.12–17 Luke 15.1–10 HC Ps 88.9–15	MP 25 EP 27 DP 92
Friday	1 March P(La)w David, bishop, patron of Wales (see p.66)	Genesis 37.3–4, 12–13, 17–28 Psalm 105.16–22 Matthew 21.33–43, 45–46	Genesis 43.1–15 1 Corinthians 7.1–9	Song of the Three vv 1–14 or Hosea 6.1–6 Luke 15.11–end HC Ps 104.26–32	MP 39 EP 69 DP 69
Saturday	2 March P(La)w Chad, bishop, missionary (see p.67)	Micah 7.14–15, 18–20 Psalm 103.1–4, 9–12 Luke 15.1–3, 11–end	Genesis 43.16–end 1 Corinthians 7.10–24	Micah 6.1–8 Luke 16.1–13 HC Ps 19.7–10	MP 13, 124 EP 31 DP 13

it is worth being prepared for a pause, just in case! If in doubt, stay quiet: there is nothing worse than confidently launching into the second half of a verse and hearing your voice echoing around on its own. Not all the psalms lend themselves to being said in this way; others may suit being said by individuals taking a verse each, or everyone saying the psalm together. They can also be sung, and the same comments apply here as for the canticles. Above all make the psalms an act of worship and prayer.

The Notes

This introductory section to the whole of *Common Worship: Daily Prayer* is probably the most valuable resource it contains. It needs little explanation, just the advice to read, mark, learn and inwardly digest. The Introduction opens up the different possibilities and patterns of prayer encouraged by *Common Worship: Daily Prayer*, and the General Notes (pp. xii–xiii) give permission for flexibility and local usage. Most helpful for those who get lost in the Church's year are the Seasonal Notes (pp. xiv–xv) which tell you which office to use when. The Calendar gives the names of the Sundays in seasons and Ordinary Time, and the dates of the Major and Lesser Festivals and Commemorations (and a tip on which is which). It is always more tempting to start building the flat-pack furniture rather than read the manual, but be boring and read the Notes!

The Lectionary

The current Weekday Lectionary is only authorized until 2004. This is to allow it to be worked through and used in full, so that mistakes and clashes will emerge, and to provide a period of experimentation to see whether its broad principles are a help or a hindrance to the Church as a whole. That is why the Lectionary is not printed in *Common Worship: Daily Prayer* and is only available in the annual lectionary booklets.

There are three patterns of Bible reading in the Lectionary as it stands. The *Eucharistic Lectionary* comprises two short sequential readings, from the Old Testament or Epistles and the Gospels. Verses from a psalm are provided which resonate with the first reading. It is familiar as the Eucharistic Lectionary from the ASB, but now dovetails more neatly with the Sunday Lectionary. This lectionary is best used for a daily Eucharist, as using it infrequently means that the readings will occur out of context: you needed to be there yesterday to understand them! (A regular weekly, rather than daily, Eucharist will be better served by the Second Office Lectionary – see below.)

The *Office Lectionary* has two longer sequential readings, from the Old and New Testaments, and will be familiar in feel to those used to a pattern of readings which aims to cover the whole Bible in a particular period of time. With some small omissions, the Office Lectionary covers the whole Bible over two years. The readings can be split over morning and evening if you wish to have just one reading at each office. The alternative is to use the Second Office Lectionary for the readings at one of the offices.

The *Second Office Lectionary* is a new departure for the Church of England. It provides a series of readings for use at an office where the congregation or clientele changes every day. The readings are designed to stand alone and do not require attendance the day before or day after in order to make sense. This might suit a cathedral evensong, for example, or a place where people come regularly but only once or twice a week. It has three possible functions:

- It can provide readings for a once-a-day office at which the congregation varies from day to day.

- If you have two offices, it can provide the readings for one of them.

- It also provides readings suitable for a weekly Eucharist. A Gospel reading is provided, where necessary, as an alternative second reading.

Choose your lectionary with care! A regular group praying in the morning might choose the Office Lectionary and enjoy the unfolding of a story or theme. A group praying once a week might choose the Second Office Lectionary and hear a clear message from discrete passages of Scripture. Another group, meeting regularly but having a Eucharist on occasions might choose the Eucharistic Lectionary as a way of reading the Bible in sequence while hearing the proclamation of Christ in the Gospels. Another group might use the office for prayer and praise, and choose the short readings found in Prayer During the Day. Choose, and reflect, and allow the Bible to speak in its different ways. It is, in the end, our greatest resource.

6 Beyond words
Gilly Myers

One thing that should be clear by now is that *Common Worship: Daily Prayer* gives wide scope for individual and local choice. Making such choices well, however, is only the beginning. The words on the page give shape and form, and they connect us with other praying communities and individuals; but the words also need to *come to life*.

It makes complete sense that we, who have been crafted in the image of a creative God, should seek creative ways of worshipping. In its notes and rubrics, *Common Worship: Daily Prayer* itself contains suggestions for the use of space, symbols, singing, movement and silence, amongst other things.

In this chapter we shall be looking at some of these possibilities as we explore ways of praying that move beyond the expression of words alone. What follows is intended to be a catalyst, not a comprehensive user manual. It is here to stir and encourage imaginative thinking in the hope that you will take advantage of your freedom to find ways of your own to enrich daily prayer.

Setting the scene

We pray in many different contexts: at home or in the office, in a small group in someone's house, in the parish church, on the train, in a religious community, at a conference . . . whatever the context, a well-set scene can do wonders for our ability to engage with, and receive from, God.

Space

It often helps to have a regular place for daily prayer. Some people have homes large enough for a permanent 'chapel' area in a small room or a corner of a room; others with less space find that making a habit of sitting in a particular armchair helps them to concentrate on the task in hand.

It is easier to find or create dedicated space for daily prayer in a church building – and there is something very significant about praying in a place that has been prayed in for centuries, if the building is an ancient one.

The physical environment

There are other considerations that can make a big difference.

- What furniture will you use? Will there be a lectern, pews, chairs, cushions, kneeling stools or hassocks?

- Is there a clear focal point? A simple cross, a candle or an open Bible can help us to focus on God.

- It is possible to use lighting to help: brightness in the morning (all the lights on) and shadowy softness at night, building up with the lighting of the lamps (see below, in the section about symbolism).

- And don't forget the temperature: could the place do with a bit more heating?

Distractions

All the best advice is usually to find a space without distractions, though in a busy world some interruptions are inevitable. Sometimes, however, these 'distractions' can be incorporated into worship. A city-centre church, for instance, might have a great deal of traffic noise or hustle and bustle beyond the doors during midday prayer. This can either become an annoyance or, more positively, a spur and reminder to pray for the life of the city.

Sounds and Silence

Daily prayer in *Common Worship* – at least as a corporate event – is not usually a silent activity. There are parts for the leader and there are congregational responses and refrains. This much is clear from the text on the page. Yet there is more that you can do with sound – and silence – to enhance a time of prayer.

Vocal variations

Invite a variety of people to speak and lead at different points

A number of voices (even two) can stimulate attentiveness, as well as giving people a greater chance to contribute. The Introduction to Morning and Evening Prayer in *Common Worship: Daily Prayer* gives the following advice:

> The character of the services as a liturgical celebration can be enhanced in a number of ways ... by assigning different parts of the service (for example, reading the Scriptures, singing the verses of psalms and canticles, leading the prayers) to different members of the worshipping group.

Incorporate singing where possible and appropriate

Morning Prayer held so early that your voice hasn't woken up, or with a group of people who cannot hold a note between them, might indicate that singing would be better left to another occasion. But people don't need to be accompanied by a full-blown choir to make the most of the psalms and canticles which, after all, are songs intended to be sung.

> Whenever possible, the services should include some singing, especially of the Gospel canticle, which is the climax of the morning or evening praise for the work of God in Christ.
> *Introduction to Morning and Evening Prayer*

The introduction to Morning and Evening Prayer in *Common Worship: Daily Prayer* makes it very clear that metrical paraphrases (hymns or songs based on the same text) may be substituted for *any* of the biblical canticles. This leaves tremendous scope for finding something that is singable. There are a number of ways of singing the psalms: either all together, or using someone with a good voice (acting as 'cantor') to give a lead with solo sections, leaving the congregation to join in with refrains. Metrical paraphrases can be found with relative ease (simply use the index of Bible references in a hymn-book).

As well as the psalms and canticles, any appropriate hymns and songs can be included in the service. The 'Praise' section in Prayer During the Day gives scope for half an hour's singing, if that would be appropriate. It is also worth looking at some of the traditional office hymns (such as those found in *Hymns for Prayer and Praise*, Canterbury Press, 1996).

But we haven't got an organist/pianist/musician . . .

Take courage. Choose simple, tuneful music and sing unaccompanied. After a bit of experience everyone will gain confidence.

What if I am on my own?

Lots of people sing around the house even though they wouldn't dream of performing in front of anybody else. There is no reason why you should not sing – unless, for example, you happen to be praying at your desk in the lunch hour, or travelling in public! It is also worth bearing in mind that reading parts of the service aloud can also enhance our prayer time, even when we are on our own. There is quite a difference between reading internally something that someone else has written and proclaiming it aloud on our own behalf.

Pre-recorded music

- Have something playing as people arrive that will help them to adjust to the focus on prayer and praise.

- Play reflective music at points where people are given some space for personal prayer and reflection.

- Play music as a background to some of the spoken parts of liturgy (such as the reading of a psalm).

- If you really can't summon up the confidence to sing unaccompanied, then try singing along to one of the many compilations of favourite hymns and songs.

Silence is golden

One frequent comment about *Common Worship* is that it has given us more words, when what we need is fewer words and more space. The point is misinformed, for the intention behind *Common Worship* (declared in its notes and rubrics) is that silence (and action, movement and symbolism) should be an integral part of worship. *Common Worship: Daily Prayer* shares this intention and, while offering a tremendous range of resources, it also encourages the use of silence and reflection.

The following are obvious possibilities:

- Before the service or office begins

- Before the confession (if it is used)

- After the reading(s)

- During the prayers.

Using the psalm prayers

In *Common Worship: Daily Prayer* each of the psalms from the *Common Worship* Psalter has been given a short concluding prayer, which draws together some of the themes of the psalm and offers them to God in a Christian context. It is best used by allowing some stillness after the psalm. This silent prayer is then gathered up by the Psalm Prayer (which is, for this reason, sometimes called a 'Psalm Collect').

When [the psalm prayers] are used, it is desirable that a period of silence for individual reflection and prayer be kept at the end of the psalm, before the prayer itself is used.

Introduction to the Psalter in Common Worship: Daily Prayer

Night Prayer

Special care needs to be given to Night Prayer so that it can be the quiet, reflective service which is intended. In addition to silence at the points already suggested, the service has a most effective ending if it concludes in silence (or with quiet music), so that the group or congregation disperses into the night without further conversation or sound. To achieve this the leader may need to give clear guidance before the service begins.

Personal prayer in a corporate context

Some of those who join public services of daily prayer will have already had the opportunity to pray and read the Bible on their own. For others, the daily prayer service may be their only time of prayer in that day. Silence can be one way of allowing for a personal expression of faith within a corporate context.

Careful leaders will leave ample space for expressing in silence the agony of failing to keep to God's paths, the personal longings of the heart, detailed prayer for events planned for the day, and time for God's word to sink in and settle. Anyone who has come to pray but leaves frustrated after a torrent of words has been cheated of an important encounter with God.

Studying the Bible within daily prayer

We have already seen that Prayer During the Day can function as a prayerful framework for extended study and reflection on the Word of God.

Commercially produced Bible reading notes can be a help with this. Most Christian bookshops stock a variety of schemes, some more 'in-depth' than others, some containing a touch of critical study, some with a devotional thought, some for young people, some which work their way through chunks of the Bible, others which dot around from day to day on a series of themes. They sometimes come with a built-in response or final prayer, which can be fed into the liturgical structure of any of the *Common Worship: Daily Prayer* offices. Bible reading notes can be used both by individuals and groups. In the latter case, the notes could be read aloud as a stimulus to, or conclusion of, a time of open or silent reflection. Sometimes a 'devotional commentary' can be used in a similar way – ask for advice at your local Christian bookshop.

Non-biblical readings

It is possible to supplement the reading of Scripture with other, non-biblical, readings which complement the readings from the Bible within the context of daily prayer. Such material is specifically suggested for inclusion where it fits most comfortably – in the Vigil Office, a reflective adaptation of Evening Prayer in preparation for a Sunday or Principal Feast:

> *A Vigil may be kept less formally; those present participate by contributing readings and poetry, music and song, testimony and prayer.*
>
> Rubric at the beginning of the Vigil Office

There may be other times, however, when supplementary non-biblical material would be helpful. During Lent, for example, you may decide to dip into some spiritual classics or follow the life of a contemporary martyr by reading from a biography. Saints' Days, Feasts, Festivals and Commemorations present other golden opportunities to be challenged or encouraged by an essay, a sermon, a short biographical summary, or a poem. Useful collections of suitable readings can be found in *Celebrating the Seasons* and *Celebrating the Saints* compiled by Robert Atwell (Canterbury Press).

Symbols in worship

A symbol is a word, action or picture that connects with something inside us and evokes a response on many different levels. Sometimes a symbol will speak to us of significant truths or express something for us that we are unable to articulate in any other way. For this reason, symbols can be of immense importance to worshippers wanting to interpret or communicate a reality which is beyond the ability of words to utter.

The Reformers of the sixteenth century were suspicious of an over-use of symbols, especially when they considered that the symbol had become a focus of superstition. More recently, however, the Church of England has been rediscovering the value of a broader range of symbols in worship when used with care. It is also interesting to note an increased desire in our society more generally to use symbols (candles, flowers, teddy-bears and suchlike) when words seem to be inadequate.

Images, pictures and icons

Images and icons can draw us into a deeper understanding, or set us off in new directions, as we seek to connect with God. Traditional Eastern iconography is based on a combination of artistic conventions, each constructed to express a particular theological point. It is carefully thought out and has a certain stylized feel to it, and it has become increasingly appreciated in recent years in the West. But there is no reason why we cannot look for contemporary art or photography that can similarly motivate and enthuse us to pray.

The character of the services as a liturgical celebration can be enhanced in a number of ways, including … the provision of a visual focus for worship, such as a cross, an icon or a lighted candle (the latter especially in the evening) …
Introduction to Morning and Evening Prayer

Such symbols need not be unvarying; a particular focus may be right only for a season or a day. Here are some suggestions.

General symbols

The cross

An emblem both of Christ's passion and of his victory over death, the cross is a powerful focus of prayer and worship. A moderately sized cross standing on a small table, or a palm-sized cross held in the hand, helps us to draw close to the one who died and lives for us.

The Bible

The Bible is, of course, a core element of daily prayer. It can be put on a lectern or a central table, for example, perhaps brought in and placed there at the beginning of the Preparation, opened in anticipation of what is to come.

A candle

Candles can be used in different ways:

- As a simple focus. Lighting a single candle or three candles (perhaps of differing heights or sizes) at the beginning of the office can be an aid to concentration on Christ, the light of the world – as well as being a clear indication that the time of prayer has begun.

- At The Blessing of Light – an ancient tradition of lighting candles or lamps as dusk falls. *Common Worship: Daily Prayer* has a form (p. 84) which can be used instead of the Preparation at Evening Prayer. A single lamp or candle is lit at the very beginning, after which those gathered hear a verse from Psalm 27, say the opening greeting and respond together to the prayer of blessing/thanksgiving. Then, as the group or congregation sings the Phos Hilaron (or something similar) other lamps or candles may be lit around the room or building.

  If The Blessing of Light is used as preparation for the Vigil Office (p. 291), the paschal candle is specifically mentioned as the one that might be brought in or lit at the beginning.

- Taizé style. The prayer area could be decorated with dozens of burning candles in transparent pots of many colours, to create a special atmosphere before people arrive.

- During the Intercessions. A large bowl of sand can be placed in a central position within the prayer space. At the Intercessions, individuals can light a votive candle and place it in the sand. An alternative would be to use a votive candle stand.

- When praying for the world, small tea-lights can be placed on a giant map of the world, laid out on the floor. (Borrow a sturdy plastic one from a local mission partner, or draw one on an old sheet with fabric pens – maybe the Junior Church can help, too.)

- Prayer for the Church's unity. *Common Worship: Daily Prayer* has a form of Prayers for the Unity of the Church which can replace the Prayers and Conclusion at Morning or Evening Prayer. The rubrics at the beginning of this say:

> *These prayers may take place around a unity candle . . .*

Franciscan communities say these prayers gathered around a central candle (the so-called unity candle) each Thursday morning, and the candle is left burning throughout the rest of the day until Night Prayer; all their prayers each Thursday are directed towards the theme of the visible unity of Christ's Church here on earth. Some cathedrals and churches have a similar custom.

- At Night Prayer. A candle, or candles, in a room or church can quieten people and heighten the sense of the surrounding darkness.

Incense

Psalm 141, used in The Blessing of Light (an optional form of Preparation for Evening Prayer) has the following refrain:

> **Let my prayer rise before you as incense,** ♦
> **the lifting up of my hands as the evening sacrifice.**
> *Psalm 141.2*

It is hardly surprising, then, that the rubrics suggest that we might burn incense at the same time.

You don't have to own a fancy brass thurible to burn incense. Simply half-fill a pottery bowl with sand, place some glowing charcoal on the sand and scatter some grains of incense on the charcoal (take care – the whole bowl can get extremely hot). The bowl could be carried in at the appropriate point.

During the prayers of intercession later in the office, anyone could take a small pinch of incense (one or two grains) and toss them onto the charcoal while they are praying.

Stones and pebbles

These can represent certain people or events 'held' in our hands before God, or they can be placed into a cairn (a 'significant' pile of stones) as a symbol of prayers being drawn together and left with God.

Clay pots

Somebody once described our human part in God's plan as being an empty clay pot. We offer the pot and ask God to fill it. An empty pot can be a symbol of our prayers, available for God to fill with his power and his desires.

Art and artists

Many churches have pieces of 'art' scattered around the building, some lurking in the shadows or hidden in a corner. Many churches also have artists and other creative people around – some of them also lurking in the shadows! Be on the lookout for people or things that can enhance daily prayer.

Contemporary photographs

It is not uncommon to enter a church building and be confronted with a photograph of a link mission partner from overseas. Some churches have full-scale picture galleries, displaying a bank of smiling staff and officers of the church. If your church has anything like this, then you may already have the beginnings of a visual prayer aid. Photographs of people for whom we pray regularly can be kept as an alternative to a written list in our prayer area or – if we pray at home – put on a notice board or in a small photo album, dedicated to prayer pictures.

You can also look out for other pictures and images that inspire you to pray. There are commercially produced resources that supply such photographic images. An example of this is *Dear*

Life, published by Christian Aid (Janet Morley, Hannah Ward and Jennifer Wild, 1998), which combines a yearly cycle of descriptions and prayers with vivid images of the people for whom the prayers are written.

Seasonal symbols

The suggestions that follow are the bare bones of symbolic ideas that can be fleshed out in your own situation. Mostly, they are ideas for short-term focal points for a particular liturgical season.

Ideas for Advent

- Symbols of 'waiting'

  ➤ A very large hour glass (one that goes on for longer than the service or prayer time would be ideal)

  ➤ An image of pregnancy

  ➤ An image of a watch-tower

- A Jesse Tree could be created throughout Advent. This is a bare tree (Christmas tree or large tree-shaped twig) which is gradually decorated with hanging symbols representing characters and events that are associated with the coming Messiah. Symbols might include an apple for Adam, a rainbow for Noah, a sky full of stars on a little picture for Abraham, a ladder made of small sticks for Jacob and so on. One symbol could be hung on the tree at the end of the Preparation each day with a few words of explanation.

- A simple plant arrangement of flowering cacti in a bed of sand cf. A Song of the Wilderness.

The wilderness and the dry land shall rejoice, ♦
The desert shall blossom and burst into song . . .

For waters shall break forth in the wilderness, ♦
And streams in the desert . . .

A Song of the Wilderness, vv. 1 and 7

- Building upon the same canticle, you could construct a sand and water feature in the place where you pray. Indoor water pumps are easy to obtain these days – someone could have an enjoyable afternoon putting it all together.

Ideas for Christmas

- Use your Nativity scene:

  ➤ Put it in the part of church where daily prayer takes place.

  ➤ Or move your prayer area for a season to the place where the crib sits, so that it can be a focus of prayer for a few weeks.

  ➤ If you pray at home but don't have a crib, consider making one from simple materials.

- Put together a display of 'Angels'.

- Display an image of the rising sun and use the second canticle regularly at Morning Prayer:

> The people who walked in darkness have seen a great light; ♦
> those who dwelt in a land of deep darkness,
> upon them the light has dawned.
>
> *A Song of the Messiah, v. 1*

- As an act of prayer, as well as an aid, make a collage from magazines and newspapers and give a contemporary interpretation to the theme of a vulnerable baby in the midst of a hostile world.

- Display an icon of the Virgin and her child.

Ideas for Epiphany

- A hanging star.

- Another water feature suggestion – this time incorporating jars, water and wine (for the Wedding at Cana in John 2.1-11, a traditional Epiphany theme).

- A jug of water next to a carafe of wine.

- A symbol of the magi. Three strips of richly coloured satin cloth can be draped over stools of varying heights and decorated with flowers and symbolic ornaments, such as gold crowns and eastern vessels.

- Symbols of the gifts: gold, frankincense and myrrh.

- If you didn't use an image of the rising sun in the Christmas season, it would be fitting for Epiphany mornings, too . . .

From the rising of the sun to its setting
your glory is proclaimed in all the world.
Preparation at Morning Prayer in Epiphany

Arise, shine out, for your light has come, ♦
the glory of the Lord is rising upon you . . .

The nations will come to your light, ♦
and kings to your dawning brightness.
A Song of the New Jerusalem, vv. 1 and 4

Old Testament Canticle at Morning Prayer in Epiphany

Ideas for Lent

- Create a display incorporating stones, bread, sackcloth and sand.

- Drape torn garments over a worn wooden chair.

- Darken your environment. Use fewer lights, or pray in a part of the building that isn't sunny, for a contrast.

- The opening canticle in Morning Prayer (Psalm 51) and the Preparation in Evening Prayer both contain 'cleansing' metaphors. Feature a washing bowl, a jug of water and a towel during Lent. This could also connect with the foot-washing on Maundy Thursday if you use the same objects.

- Display images of . . .

  ➤ sorrow, lament and suffering

  ➤ darkness

  ➤ fire (for the 'purging' metaphors)

Ideas for Passiontide

- Place a large metal nail in a prominent place, or give each member of the group one to hold or look at. It is possible to buy 2 inch and 3 inch nails in a traditional shape, with a square end, which look more authentic.

- Much can be done with a large wooden cross (or a small one, if a large one is impractical)

  ➤ These are the introductions to the Lord's Prayer in Morning and Evening Prayer during Passiontide:

Standing at the foot of the cross,
as our Saviour has taught us, so we pray
Our Father in heaven ...
                                        Contemporary language

Standing at the foot of the cross,
let us pray with confidence as our Saviour has taught us
Our Father, who art in heaven ...
                                        Traditional language

Why not gather around the cross and stand there for the prayers (or move to the cross for just the Lord's Prayer)?

➤ Intercessions could be written on pieces of paper and attached to the cross during Passiontide.

➤ In a special act of penitence – perhaps on Good Friday – confessions could be pinned onto the cross (NB careful planning will be necessary for the disposal of these papers, owing to their confidential nature).

➤ Prayers at the Foot of the Cross. *Common Worship: Daily Prayer* includes an optional section called Prayers at the Foot of the Cross at the end of the Morning and Evening Prayer section of the book (p. 283); it can replace the Prayers and the Conclusion in these services. This form of prayer is not only for Good Friday; it is recommended for any Friday or appropriate occasion.

> *A procession may be made towards a suitable cross, before which lights may be burning, or a cross may be carried in. It may be mounted upright or laid on the ground, with lights burning around it.*

The people may wish to gather around the cross at this point, to pray, or they may wish to come up to it one by one . . .

> *While silence is kept, or appropriate hymns or chants are sung, any of those present may come forward to touch the cross. They may, for example, place their forehead on it as a sign of entrusting to God, in union with Christ and his suffering, their own burdens as well as those of others.*
>
> *Other forms of intercessions may be offered.*

People may also wish to kneel for some time in prayer around the cross, and it would be helpful to place a few hassocks around the area to encourage this to happen.

- Give a statue of a pelican a prominent place in the prayer area. The maternal pelican is a long-standing symbol of Christ, as one who sheds her own blood in order that others might live; she is known to pluck her breast and draw blood with which to nourish her young. This symbol might need some explanation when it is first introduced.

Ideas for Easter

- The Easter garden. Such a garden can become the site of daily prayer for all or part of the Easter season.

- The paschal candle. If the church has a paschal candle, first lit on Easter Day to symbolize the light of the risen Christ, perhaps it could be moved somewhere for daily prayer so that it can also be an effective focus for smaller weekday services.

- The transformed cross. The section of ideas for Good Friday and Passiontide, above, concentrated very much on the cross of the crucifixion, the cross of suffering and death. By contrast, the cross of Easter is one of victory and hope.

  Perhaps there are imaginative ways of transforming the cross you used during the devotions of the preceding weeks. Bright, ornate crosses, previously muted underneath Lenten coverings, will be revealed in shining splendour once again; wooden crosses adorned with nails, crowns of thorns and purple cloth may, instead, be decorated from head to foot with bright flowers and foliage or Easter lilies.

- Display an image of the empty tomb.

Ideas for Ascension to Pentecost

The period between the Ascension and Pentecost is a time for praying and waiting. Praying and waiting for the Holy Spirit, just as the disciples were told to wait 'in the city (Jerusalem) until you have been clothed with power from on high' (Luke 24.49).

- Display a symbol of the Holy Spirit:
  - Dove
  - Wild Goose
  - Fire
  - Wind (quite a challenge to depict!)

Ideas for All Saints to Advent

All Saints to Advent is not, strictly speaking, a distinct season in the *Common Worship* calendar, although it may be treated as a 'Kingdom' season. There is no doubt that the mood of the year changes in this part of the world as we give thanks for the harvest, move well into autumn and feel the approach of winter. We pass through All Saints and All Souls, with the memories that they invoke, and we have another day of recollection and resolve on Remembrance Sunday. Given the themes of this 'season', ideas in this section are in part about reflection, in part about looking forward, and in part about the kingship of Jesus.

- Footsteps. We are following the Way of Christ and in the footsteps of the saints. Put cut-out 'footsteps' on the wall or floor of the prayer area (they could perhaps lead from one place to another . . .).

- Arrange a number of icons of saints all round the prayer area (a reminder of the 'great cloud of witnesses' described in Hebrews).

- Display an icon of Christ reigning in glory.

- Display a large picture of the earth or the universe for a few weeks.

Movement, posture and action

Kneeling, standing and lying prostrate are just some of the alternatives to sitting for our prayers. Arms may be outstretched or raised in prayer; hands may be open to receive from God; a dance or procession might move us round the building.

Common Worship: Daily Prayer encourages us to think about movement and posture.

The character of the services as a liturgical celebration can be enhanced in a number of ways, including the use of appropriate changes of posture and physical movement . . .
Introduction to Morning and Evening Prayer

Here are some ideas to try:

- Rethink how the prayer time begins and ends or how people arrive and leave.

- Have another look at the furniture and the way it is laid out. Does it facilitate different kinds of movement? A church that I used to attend had to pack in a lot of people. Its very comfortable new chairs were positioned so close to the ones in front that it was quite impossible to kneel down.

- Look carefully at the words. Does your posture match what you are saying?

- Set up a 'prayer station' on a particular theme. This could be a three-dimensional display or picture board, for example. During the prayers, people can gather around the station, using what they see, hear, smell or touch as a catalyst to their intercession. Here are some examples:

  ➤ An old blanket tossed on the floor by a tatty pillow and a dog-lead (indicative of homelessness).

  ➤ A series of pictures projected onto a screen from a slide projector (on any subject you choose).

  ➤ A back-drop of pictures from a dry country where the crops have failed, and a table on which there is an empty bowl and a crumpled sack. Invite people to place small tea-lights around the edges of the table as they pray.

- Gifts are usually received open-handed. Why not emulate that waiting, receptive gesture with arms open and palms uppermost during Advent or as Pentecost approaches?

- Share the Peace.

> The Peace may be exchanged at the Conclusion of any Order.
>
> *General Notes to* Common Worship: Daily Prayer

Appendix 1
Some definitions

Antiphon
A short verse used at the beginning and end of a canticle, consisting of words from the canticle or from elsewhere in the Bible. Also called a refrain. In the psalms the antiphon may occur during the psalm as well as at the beginning and the end.

Antiphonally
A way of saying (or singing) the psalms and canticles. One group of people say a verse or half a verse, and the other group replies with the other verse or half verse.

Calendar
The way the seasons and special days of the Church's year are organized. See also *Sanctorale* and *Temporale*.

Canticle
Literally meaning 'little song', a canticle is a set form of praise, usually deriving from the Bible.

Capitulum
The Latin name for a short reading, normally just a verse or two, used when the office concentrates on prayer and praise, or when sustained Bible reading takes place at another time of the day.

Collect
A short prayer, following a set pattern, used at the end of the Gathering at Holy Communion, and at the end of Intercession in daily prayer. The Collect set for Sundays has often been used as the 'prayer of the week' in the Church of England.

Common (of the Saints)
Special material used in daily prayer when remembering a saint.

Some saints have their own material; the rest have material 'common' to them.

Hours of Prayer
The set times of prayer kept by monastic communities.

Invitatory
The opening canticle of Morning and Evening Prayer.

Lectionary
A pattern of Bible readings ('lections'), organized over a defined period of time. *Common Worship* has lectionaries for Sundays and for weekdays. The term 'lectionary' can also refer to the booklet which contains the tables of Bible references for the year, or to a book containing the readings printed out in full.

Office
The general term for regular, organized daily prayer, normally containing set forms of praise, prayer and Bible reading, and occurring more than once in the day. From the Latin term *officium*, meaning service or duty. Also referred to as the Daily Office.

Ordinary Time
The part of the Church's year where no special theme predominates: roughly the time between Pentecost and Advent and between the Presentation of Christ (2 February – sometimes called 'Candlemas') and Ash Wednesday. Sometimes called the 'Green Season', after the liturgical colour used at this time.

Propers
Special material, including *antiphons, responsories* and *collects*, used at particular times of the Church's year, or on particular holy days. These texts are 'properly' used on those days, and the shorthand is to call them the 'propers'.

Responsory
Words of Scripture used at the end of a Bible reading, taking the form of a versicle and response.

Responsorially
A way of saying or singing the psalms. The refrain is said or sung by everyone, with one voice saying or singing the verses of the psalm. Everyone joins in the refrain at the points indicated.

Rubric
A liturgical instruction or piece of advice. Rather like a stage direction in a play. Called a rubric because in early prayer books they were written in red, to distinguish them from texts which were to be said.

Sanctorale
The part of the Calendar that defines the dates of holy days and special festivals.

Seasons
Parts of the Church's year where special themes or events in the life of Christ and the Church are remembered. These are: Advent; Christmas; Epiphany; Lent (including Holy Week); and Easter (including Ascension to Pentecost). *Common Worship* suggests that the period between All Saints' Day and the First Sunday of Advent, though not strictly a 'season', can be used to remember the reign of Christ in earth and heaven.

Temporale
The part of the Calendar that defines Ordinary Time and the seasons of the year.

Appendix 2
The legal position concerning Daily Prayer

There are some legalities which need to be taken into account when thinking about Daily Prayer. Canon C26 'Of the Manner of life of ministers' states that 'Every bishop, priest, and deacon is under obligation, not being let by sickness or some other urgent cause, to say daily the Morning and Evening Prayer, either privately or openly . . .'. Canon B11 'Of Morning and Evening Prayer in parish churches' states that 'the minister of the parish, together with other ministers licensed to serve in the parish, shall make such provision for Morning and Evening Prayer to be said or sung either in the parish church or . . . elsewhere as may best serve to sustain the corporate spiritual life of the parish and the pattern of life enjoined upon ministers by Canon C26. Public notice shall be given in the parish by tolling the bell or other appropriate means . . . .' Canon B14 A gives some flexibility to this, allowing the saying of Morning and Evening Prayer to be dispensed with on an occasional or even regular basis, but only after appropriate consultation, including consultation with the bishop.

In other words, all clergy are obliged to say Morning and Evening Prayer, and all parochial clergy are required to provide Morning and Evening Prayer in parishes, giving appropriate notice of time and venue. A daily pattern should only be dispensed with by agreement between the clergy, the PCC and the bishop.

This is not the place to take issue with the Canons, except to observe that strict adherence to all their provisions is probably more the exception than the norm across the Church of England. What concerns us here is what may be used as 'Morning' and

'Evening' Prayer so that the canonical obligation might be fulfilled.

In the Church of England the controlling document for worship is *The Book of Common Prayer*. Contemporary forms of service introduced in recent years have not superseded the BCP, but provide alternatives to it. If a form of service is provided in the BCP, then any equivalent contemporary form of service has to be authorized by the General Synod. So, for instance, because the Prayer Book includes a service of Holy Communion, the *Common Worship* Holy Communion services have to be authorized as alternatives to it. If, on the other hand, a contemporary service has no counterpart in the BCP, then it needs no authorization. This is because the canons already provide that, for services for which there is no Prayer Book form, the minister may use forms of service which are 'reverent and seemly' and consistent with Church of England doctrine (see Canon B5). In recent years such forms of service provided by the Liturgical Commission have simply been 'commended' by the House of Bishops as suitable (but not compulsory) forms. (For example, much of the seasonal material found in *The Promise of His Glory*, CHP 1991, falls into this 'commended' category.)

The authorized alternative to the BCP's Morning and Evening Prayer is A Service of the Word. This is unique in the Church of England's liturgy in that it is not a complete text, but is rather a set of headings and notes. They can be found on pp. 21–7 of *Common Worship: Services and Prayers for the Church of England*. A Service of the Word requires certain elements to be included in a service, but leaves open how these elements are chosen, and allows a variety of texts to be used. Morning and Evening Prayer as printed in *Common Worship: Daily Prayer* fulfils the requirements of the Canons in that it conforms to the provisions of A Service of the Word. However, a worshipper keen to obey the Canons and use an authorized service need not follow *Common Worship: Daily Prayer* slavishly, and, to take a ridiculous example, it would still be legal (though not sensible) to use the Advent order in Pentecost!

Moreover, the texts on the pages of *Common Worship: Daily Prayer* are not the only way of conforming to A Service of the Word. There is a great deal of flexibility built into the requirements. The only parts of the service requiring a restricted number of texts are Prayers of Penitence and the Creed, neither of which have to be used on weekdays. Therefore *Celebrating Common Prayer* is brought into the legal fold, as are many other publications. It is worth checking your favourite publication against the rules of A Service of the Word, which now acts as the 'controlling' authorization for a great variety of provisions. That said, a sense of Anglican commonality might steer those for whom daily prayer is both a duty and a joy to explore the depth and breadth of *Common Worship: Daily Prayer* before venturing further afield!

The Psalter and the Bible

Any translation of the Psalms may be used for Daily Prayer: the *Common Worship* Psalter is simply the version approved by the Synod to be printed with *Common Worship* services. Any translation of the Bible not prohibited by the Versions of the Bible Measure may be used in authorized alternative services. As yet no translation of the Bible is prohibited! (Note, however, that, in the Lectionary, verse numbers for the psalms follow the *Common Worship* Psalter and for other readings follow the New Revised Standard Version.)

Notes

Introduction

1. *The Divine Office*, Collins, 1974, compilation copyright © Roman Catholic hierarchies of England and Wales, Ireland, Australia.
2. Perhaps the most readable book on the subject at present is by George Guiver CR, *Company of Voices*, SPCK, revised edition 2001. Another definitive work is Robert Taft's *The Liturgy of the Hours in East and West*, second revised edition 1993, Liturgical Press.
3. *Benedict of Nursia, The Rule*, translated by Owen Chadwick.
4. Ibid.
5. Guiver, op. cit., pp. 119, 121.

Chapter 1: A living tradition of daily prayer

1. How this might be put into practice using the rich provision of *Common Worship: Daily Prayer* is the subject of Appendix 2, which looks at the legal issues in detail.

Chapter 2: Using Prayer During the Day

1. See for example *The Book of Alternative Services of the Anglican Church of Canada*, Anglican Book Centre, Toronto, 1985, and *A New Zealand Prayer Book*, Collins, 1989.
2. *Hymns for Prayer and Praise*, Canterbury Press, 1996.
3. Though note that no alternatives are offered when the Psalms of Ascent occur in the Weekday Lectionary for Morning or Evening Prayer.
4. Easily accessible collections can be found in Angela Ashwin, *Woven into Prayer*, Canterbury Press, 1999; Paul Sheppey (ed.), *Each Day, Each Night*, Canterbury Press, 1997, and *Celebrating Common Prayer, The Pocket Version*, Mowbray, 1994.

Chapter 3: Morning and Evening Prayer

1. If you want to get very pedantic, because Morning and Evening Prayer is based on *A Service of the Word*, you can actually include anything which conforms to the requirements of *A Service of the Word*, and use none of this material at all. See Appendix 2 for more details. However, Morning and Evening Prayer in *Common Worship: Daily Prayer* has its own integrity, and that (I assume) is why the word 'required' is used, rather than 'mandatory'.
2. *The Promise of His Glory*, Church House Publishing, 1991.
3. Canticles are explored further in Chapter 5, p. 79.
4. During the Reformation there was some objection to canticles of any form, on the basis that in the Bible only the psalms are clearly songs of worship. This is the reason why there are psalms offered as alternatives to the canticles in *The Book of Common Prayer*, first seen in the Prayer Book of 1552.
5. Both uses can be found in the Eucharist in *Common Worship*. The Collect ends The Gathering (e.g. p. 171, *Common Worship: Services and Prayers for the Church of England*) and Collects to end the Intercessions are provided in the Supplementary Texts, pp. 288–289 in *Common Worship: Services and Prayers for the Church of England*.

Chapter 5: Using the resource sections

1. See R. C. D. Jasper and Paul Bradshaw, *A Companion to the Alternative Service Book*, SPCK, 1986, p. 75ff., for a survey of the history, and Paul Bradshaw, *Two Ways of Praying*, SPCK, 1995 for an accessible introduction.
2. Technically called 'antiphons', they were also attached to the psalms and made use of short verses taken from psalms or other pieces of scripture. When the office was sung, the antiphon sung by the cantor defined which tune would be used. Some antiphons became very elaborate, especially those used in procession.
3. A detailed introduction to the *Common Worship* Psalter can be found in Paul Bradshaw (ed.), *Companion to Common Worship*, SPCK, 2001, pp. 236–41).

Index